VW Beetle
Performance Handbook

Keith Seume

motorbooks

First published in 1997 by Motorbooks, an imprint of MBI Publishing Company, 400 First Avenue North, Suite 300, Minneapolis, MN 55401 USA

Motorbooks titles are also available at discounts in bulk quantity for industrial or sales-promotional use. For details write to Special Sales Manager at MBI Publishing Company, 400 First Avenue North, Suite 300, Minneapolis, MN 55401 USA.

To find out more about our books, join us online at www.motorbooks.com.

ISBN-13: 978-0-7603-0469-3

Printed in China

On the front cover, main: Jay Myers of Battlefield, Missouri, built this 1956 Cal-look VW Beetle from a $150 junkyard hulk. Every part of the '56 is revamped, including the extensively-modified, narrowed front suspension using KYB adjustable gas shocks and HD swaybar. He also added 15-inch Empi five-spoke wheels and a 1968 transaxle with drop swing axle using IRS backing plates. Myers custom-built the 1973 dual port, 1,641cc flat-four with a simple induction using a Holley/Weber two-barrel on an Empi manifold, topped with an Empi air cleaner and Thunderbird exhaust. The '56 is finished off with a stunning coat of Raspberry and Violet Pearl paint. *fethers@davidfetherston.com*
Small: Building a high-performance engine for a Beetle is made possible thanks to the wide availability of specialist parts that can nearly double the horsepower of the original Volkswagen unit. Keeping it cool is another matter, but full-flow oil systems and fan cooling developed from Porsche 911 parts are the modern answer. *James Hale*

On the back cover: The detail on this show-winning customised Super Beetle is truly superb. The perfect black paint and graphics of the car's exterior has been carried on beneath the wheel arches to complement the fully-chromed MacPherson strut front suspension, brake calipers, and cross-drilled rotors. *James Hale*

Contents

Foreword

Who would have believed it? When the Volkswagen Beetle first saw the light of day over 50 years ago, few would ever have thought it would become such a cult car – and even fewer would have expected it to prove a suitable candidate for fast road use, let alone drag racing. But it's true: with a little patience, the right parts and some effort, the seemingly humble Volkswagen can be transformed into a car which handles like a sports car, goes like a Porsche (or faster) and stops on a dime.

The aim of this book is to point people in the right direction, making the VW enthusiast – newcomer and old hand alike – aware of some of the options. We shall look at the engine and how to modify it to produce reliable horsepower for use in anything from daily drivers to all-out street and strip cars; we examine the transmission and see how that can be best modified to allow you to make full use of your new-found horsepower; we show you how it is possible to make your Beetle handle like it was on rails, and we then show you how to bring everything back to rest again with as little drama as possible. Further sections look at choosing wheels and tyres, as well as listing vital pieces of information about your car.

No book like this can have been produced without the help of others, so I would like to thank the following for their assistance and support: Jacky Morel of *Super VW* magazine (France); Ivan McCutcheon at *VolksWorld* magazine (UK); Geoff Thomas at Autocavan Volksport and John Maher of John Maher Racing (both in the UK). A special word of thanks must go to Adam Wik of Wik's Racing Engines and Harold Carter at Carter's Gearbox Shop (both in the USA). Some photographs were also loaned by Scat Enterprises, Gene Berg Enterprises and Pauter Machine in the USA. I would like to thank my wife Gwynn for her help and all the Beetle enthusiasts across the world for making the VW scene what it is today.

Keith Seume
Crondall
Hampshire
England
July 1997

Analysis of the Beetle

Engines from 1100 to 1600
What the Beetle had to offer throughout its life

Built way back in 1936, this 985cc four-cylinder engine was the true forefather of the Beetle's familiar aircooled unit. It was plagued with cooling problems as no oil-cooler was fitted. Power output was just 23.5bhp.

The following year, the engine was given a new crankcase incorporating an oil-cooler. Basic design was very similar to the early 25bhp engine fitted to Beetle in the post-war years. Note cylinder head design.

Ugly, Slow, Noisy… – so went Volkswagen's legendary self-deprecating advertisements for the Beetle in the 1960s. Well, beauty (and hence ugliness) are in the eye of the beholder and surely no-one can seriously call a stock 1200 Beetle a noisy car? But slow? Well, maybe the critics did have a point.

The original design brief for the Beetle called for a car capable of transporting a family of four at a speed of 100km/h (roughly 60mph), all day, every day. That may have been fine for the 1930s, but in today's traffic a car which struggles to reach 70mph and slows down at the sight of every hill can be something of an embarrassment. However, this popular image of the Beetle is what makes modifying one such great fun. After all, nobody expects a Beetle to be able to accelerate from zero to 60mph in under 10 seconds, let alone six or seven, or reach speeds of over 120mph!

It seems almost inconceivable that an engine which produced 25bhp in its original form, later to reach the heady heights of 48bhp, could be expected to produce in excess of 150bhp and still live to tell the tale. But it's true, and power outputs of closer to 200bhp and beyond are not unknown, even where street-legal VWs are concerned. Such extreme engines are, as might be expected, expensive to build and quite beyond the reach of the average enthusiast. And to be perfectly honest, they can hardly be considered reliable daily-driver material, being better suited to quick blasts on a Friday night at the local stoplight drags. However, they are indicative of the potential lurking within every Beetle, however humble it might first appear.

In standard form, the Beetle came with a variety of engines over the years, ranging in size from the original 1131cc unit, used until December 1953, to

The classic Oval-window Beetle was the mainstay of the VW family throughout the latter part of the 1950s. Powered by the 30bhp 1192cc engine, its performance could best be described as adequate, rather than exciting.

There is no reason on earth why you shouldn't consider using a Cabriolet as a basis for building a fast street car, although you should be aware that the initial purchase price is likely to be far greater than that of an equivalent saloon.

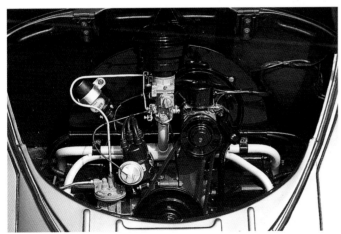

The trusty 30bhp (US 36hp) engine was fitted from 1954 until 1960. It was one of the best units ever used, being supremely reliable and relatively frugal. It was even installed in the Type 2 (bus) range with success.

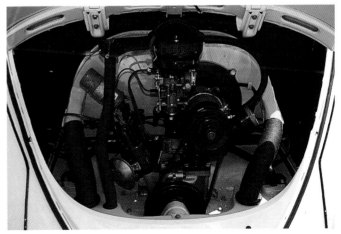

The later 34bhp (US 40hp) unit was more robust and would remain in use for over a quarter of a century. The most obvious difference between this and the earlier engine is the use of a separate, bolt-on, generator mounting.

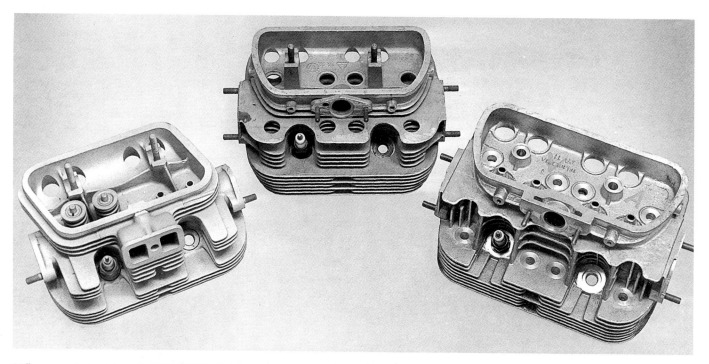

Volkswagen redesigned the cylinder head several times throughout the Beetle's life. From the left is the 1936 design (note separate inlet ports); in the center is the single-port 1945 casting; on the right is the 1960 version.

The 1938 VW38 prototype used this 985cc engine which produced 24bhp and propelled the Beetle to 105km/h (65mph). A picture of simplicity, who could have believed that one day Beetle engines would produce 200bhp, or more?

the 1584cc (1600) engine first seen in the Type 3 range in August 1965. In between are the 1192cc (1200), 1285cc (1300) and 1483cc (1500) engines. All are of horizontally-opposed, aircooled four-cylinder layout with a two-piece cast aluminium/magnesium alloy crankcase, separate cast-iron cylinders and cast aluminium cylinder heads with two valves per cylinder. The crankshaft – a high-quality forging in most instances – runs in four main bearings, while the camshaft, which is driven from the crank by way of a pair of timing gears, runs in three. Forged steel connecting rods (con-rods) feature plain white-metal big-end (rod) bearings and bronze bushes at the small-end (wrist-pin). Cast-aluminium pistons run directly in the cylinders which, unlike many other engines, have no separate liners.

The cylinder heads are one-piece castings, each including the combustion chambers for the two adjoining cylinders. A separate pressed-steel valve cover conceals the rocker assemblies, which are actuated by aluminium pushrods positioned below the cylinders. Each cylinder has one inlet and one exhaust valve, these being retained in the head by single-coil valve springs and forged steel retainers. In stock form, the springs fit directly against the cylinder head casting, located in small machined pockets to prevent them moving as the valves are opened and closed.

The valve gear itself is simple, consisting of four individual cast rocker arms which pivot on a hardened steel shaft and are located by means of hair-pin clips and spring shims. The assemblies were originally mounted directly onto the cylinder heads via cast-in pedestals designed to accept the rocker shafts, which were located with a machined clamp and nut. Later designs saw the rocker assemblies secured to the cylinder heads with steel blocks through which the shafts passed. These were held in place on each cylinder head with a pair of studs and nuts.

Throughout the years there were many changes made to the engine, ranging from relatively minor detail modifications, intended to improve longevity, to major redesigns of the cylinder head and crankcase. The 25bhp 1131cc engine fitted to Beetles until the 1954 model year was essentially the same as the 30bhp (US 36hp)1192cc unit used from then until August 1960. It consisted of a two-piece crankcase, cast from a material known as Elektron, and is most easily recognized by the integral generator-mounting pedestal. Later 34bhp (US 40hp)1192cc engines, fitted from August 1960 onwards, had a separate mounting for the generator, which was bolted in place.

The first production cylinder heads were all single-port castings, so-called because they featured a siamesed inlet port which served the two adjacent cylinders. Note the cast-in mountings for the rocker assemblies.

Dual-port head (note the separate inlet ports) was first introduced on the Type 3 range in 1968 and soon proved to be popular among VW enthusiasts in search of extra power. The new head flowed far better than any modified single-port casting.

All Beetle engines have separate cast-iron cylinders with cast aluminium pistons running directly in the bores. This design, so similar to many aero-engines, allows the capacity to be increased relatively easily, simply by changing to a larger bore.

Placed side-by-side, the single- and dual-port heads are very similar. However, note the slight variation in the design of the cooling fins either side of the inlet ports. For anyone with a 1300-1600 engine, swapping to dual-port heads is a must.

All early engines came with single-port heads – by that we mean each cylinder head featured a single siamesed inlet port serving both cylinders on that side of the engine. The design was adequate for the job in hand, limiting the breathing capabilities of the engine, and hence its output, and acting as a restrictor to prevent the engine from being over-revved. By breathing, we refer to the engine's ability to draw air and fuel in through the induction system, burn it and expel the waste through the exhaust system – the more it can 'breathe', the more power it can make. Add a restriction anywhere along the line and the power output will suffer.

With the introduction of the 1300 and 1500 engines (and indeed the first of the 1600 engines in the Type 3 and US-spec Type 1), the single-port design was retained, the size of the port being enlarged slightly to take into account the larger engines' breathing requirements. It was not until 1968 that an all-new cylinder head was introduced on the Type 3 and then, eventually, on the Beetle in August 1970, this being what is known as the twin- or dual-port head.

As the name suggests, this new head casting featured separate inlet ports for each cylinder, allowing the larger engine to breathe far better. The head was also used on the 1300 models outside the USA, and in the 1302 and 1303 ranges. Even in stock form, these dual-port heads outflowed any previous factory-produced cylinder heads, including the large-port 1500 casting, and were the answer to the hot-rodder's prayer.

In its basic form, the aircooled Volkswagen engine could never be accused of providing anything other than adequate performance when installed in a Beetle. If you bolt a stock 1600 dual-port motor into a lightweight kit car you probably won't be disappointed with the way it goes (well, not for a few weeks, anyway), but you would have to be a person of modest expectations to be impressed by a stock Beetle's ability (or lack of it) to hustle

First introduced in 1965, the 1285cc (1300) engine was a real step up from the earlier 1192cc unit. Producing a cool 40bhp (US 44hp), the new engine allowed the Beetle to cruise at a slightly higher speed with greater reliability.

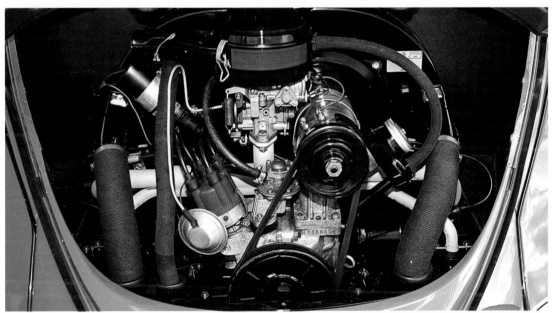

The 1500 engine was introduced in August 1966. It was a single-port unit and upheld the VW tradition of durability while offering improved performance.

Dual-port heads arrived on the Type 1 engine with the 1600 introduced in August 1970. Installing one of these units in an earlier car is the simplest way to improve performance for the minimum outlay.

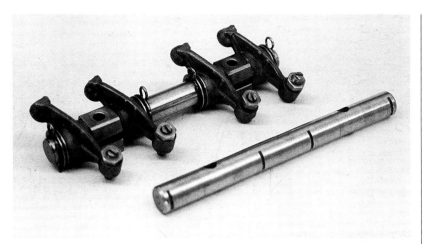

those so-called sports cars which come from the Far East. Raid the bank account, rustle up those savings and you could soon yell 'Auf Wiedersehen!' to Porsche's finest. Intrigued? Read on…

STOCK TRANSMISSIONS
From swing-axles and no synchromesh to CV-joints and high ratios

The transmission used in the Volkswagen Beetle and its brethren is an amazing piece of engineering. Originally designed to cater for no more than 50 or 60bhp, the unit has proved itself capable of handling in excess of 450bhp, albeit in somewhat modified form.

The first VW transmission – or transaxle, to give it the correct name – was a well-engineered four-speed, non-synchromesh design with the gear cluster housed in a two-piece cast alloy casing which was split lengthways, along the centerline of the car. The final drive unit consisted of a differential with spider gears and a helically-cut ring and pinion, driving two half shafts. The shafts were pivoted at the inner end so that they could move up and down

One of the weaknesses of the VW engine when used at higher rpm is the design of the rocker assemblies. The rocker arms are retained on their shaft by crude hairpin clips which are prone to failure.

The VW transmission used this high-quality casing (left) in which the gear-set and differential unit were housed. Very strong, the unit has proved capable of handling four times its intended power input. Later single-sided casing (right) is relatively uncommon.

down the freeway. If your Beetle's engine is the basic 34bhp (US 40hp) 1200, then be prepared to read every word on the back of that truck in front of you when you head for the mountains.

But it needn't always be like this for, with relatively little expenditure, it is possible to improve the performance of your basic street car without destroying any of its reliability or driveability. Spend a little more and you can be saying 'Sayonara' to

with suspension travel, giving rise to the term 'swing-axle' to describe this type of transmission.

This 'split-case' non-synchromesh transmission was used until 1953, after which it was replaced by a virtually identical unit which came with synchromesh on the top three gears (except on standard models which retained the non-synchromesh 'box). This transmission was to remain in production until 1960, when it was replaced by an all-new unit featuring a one-piece main casing, referred to as the 'tunnel' transmission. This later all-synchromesh unit became the mainstay of VW transaxles, changing very little in detail, even with the advent of the later IRS (independent rear suspension) design in 1968 (on US-specification models).

While on the subject of the later transmission, we should note that the title 'IRS' is deceiving, for it implies that the earlier swing-axle design was not fully independent, which of course it was. However, the term IRS has fallen into regular parlance and is now the accepted description for the later four-joint design (a reference to the number of constant velocity joints in the rear suspension) used in the semi-automatic and the 1302 and 1303 models. Even so, it should be noted that, other than the differential unit itself, swing-axle and IRS transmissions are virtually identical.

The biggest advantage the late tunnel transmission has over its predecessor is strength – the old split-case unit was very weak (the main problems were the pinion bearing and the straight-cut first gear) and, while adequate for use with a stock 25 or 30bhp (US 36hp) engine, it is unsuited for use with anything more potent. Actually, in some ways, that isn't strictly true, for the old split-case trans did see use in numerous VW-based sports cars during the fifties and many were even subjected to use on the drag strip in the early days of VW motorsport. However, now that there is a viable alternative which is readily available, the old-style transmission should be regarded as obsolete as far as we are concerned.

Owners of pre-1961 Beetles who wish to upgrade to the later gearbox can do so quite easily, although you may need to look around for the necessary parts. The reason a late tunnel transmission won't fit straight into an oval-window Beetle, for instance, is that the front gearbox mounting is different ('front' here refers to the front of the car). To get around this, there are two alternatives. The first is to cut off the original mounting from the chassis and weld in its place the later type (part number 111 701 073C), or a scratch-built version thereof. This is in many ways the best way to tackle the swap but it is not easy to carry out while the body is still mounted on the floorpan. If you are going the whole way and removing the bodyshell for major restoration work, then welding in the new mounting is fairly straightforward: offer the new transmission up to the

This is a swing-axle differential casing – note the large hole in the side to allow oil to lubricate the differential gears. Casing is relatively weak and will not stand too much abuse without failure. Snap ring locates in groove to retain gears.

The later IRS differential casing is far stronger (note the smaller oiling hole), although the splined output shafts are prone to breakage when used hard. Holes round circumference are for crown wheel.

car, holding it in place with the rear mounting, and align the gear selector linkage. With the 'box held in place with a jack, tack weld the new mounting to the chassis and, when you are certain it is aligned correctly and that the gear linkage works, remove the 'box and finish the welding. Incidentally, if you are solid-mounting the gearbox, which someone building a serious street-racer might be considering, then it is possible to use a commercially-available conversion bracket which allows the use of a late transmission with the early-style mounting.

The other alternative is to use the nose-cone from an early Type 2 transmission (pre-'68) and the matching 'hockey stick' gear selector rod, bolted in place of the original Beetle components. The

Beware when swapping transmissions: Volkswagen made several changes to the design of the clutch release arm and the length of the clutch cable conduit between the chassis and the gearbox. Make sure the components match your transmission.

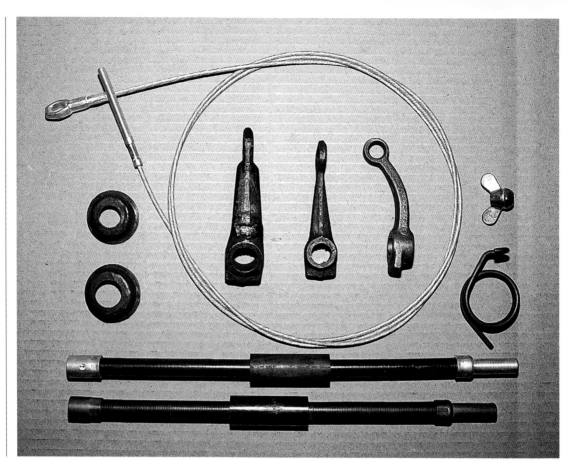

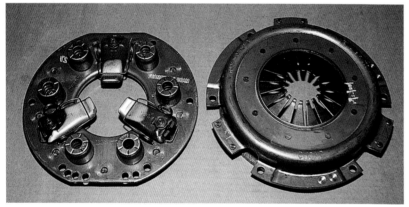

Two basic designs of clutch pressure plate have been used by Volkswagen: on the left is the spring type, while on the right is the later diaphragm design. Diaphragm type usually results in lighter pedal pressure for the same 'grab pressure'.

selector rod needs to be modified slightly – the small locating detent for the set-screw on the gear linkage coupling is drilled from underneath on a Type 2, as opposed to from above on a Beetle. This detent must therefore be redrilled 180° from its original location so that it can be used with the Beetle's coupling. This is by far the most simple way to carry out the late-into-early swap and the part numbers are 211 301 205H for the nose-cone and 113 311 541 for the selector rod. You will also need a new mounting pad, part number 211 310 265A, to complete the conversion.

The principal way in which the stock 'tunnel' transmissions differ from each other, other than whether they are from a swing-axle or IRS car, is in the matter of gear ratios. To begin with, all 1200 and 1300 models come with 4.375:1 final drive (ring and pinion) ratio, while the 1500 and most

1600s come with 4.125:1. Some late-model 1600s and Karmann Ghias came with a 3.875:1 final drive which has become very sought after, not only by people wishing to install a high-ratio transmission for better freeway cruising, but also by drag racers who appreciate the extra strength of the 3.875:1 ring and pinion.

Over the years, the ratios fitted to the various Beetle transmissions have changed, the first split-case units having the following:

1st	3.60:1
2nd	2.07:1
3rd	1.25:1
4th	0.80:1
Final drive	4.43:1 or 4.37:1

The later split-case, part-synchromesh transmission used until 1960 was equipped with the following:

1st	3.60:1	2nd	1.88:1
3rd	1.22:1	4th	0.82:1
Final drive 4.43:1			

With the introduction of the new all-synchromesh, tunnel-type transmission, the ratios were changed yet again to reflect the characteristics of the new 1200 and, later, the 1300 engine:

1st	3.80:1
2nd	2.06:1
3rd	1.32:1 (1.26 from chassis no. 116 021 298)
4th	0.89:1 (0.93 from chassis no. 113 000 001)
Final drive	4.375:1

When the 1500 model arrived in August 1966, the gear ratios were changed yet again:

1st 3.80:1
2nd 2.06:1
3rd 1.26:1
4th 0.89:1
Final drive 4.125:1

The last significant change to the transmission came in 1972 when first gear was changed slightly. This was not so much a change of ratio but an attempt to increase the strength of first gear: the old 3.80 ratio comprised a weak 10-tooth mainshaft and a 38-tooth gear, while the new 3.78:1 ratio comprised a 9-tooth mainshaft and 34-tooth gear. This may not sound like a major difference, but it is generally reckoned that the replacement gear assembly is twice as strong as its predecessor. Ratios were:

1st 3.78:1
2nd 2.06:1
3rd 1.26:1
4th 0.89:1 (0.93 from chassis no. 113 000 001)
Final drive 4.375:1 (1300), 4.125:1 (1600), 3.875:1 (some 1600 and Karmann Ghia models)

The Beetle's Suspension
Torsion bars or MacPherson struts – you have a choice

From the very beginning, Ferdinand Porsche's designs for a People's Car incorporated torsion bar suspension. A torsion bar is essentially a tempered steel bar which, when twisted at one end, acts as a rising-rate spring: the more you try to twist the bar, the stiffer it becomes. As used on the Volkswagen Beetle, torsion bar suspension gives an excellent ride regardless of whether the vehicle is lightly or heavily loaded.

The Beetle's front suspension consists of a pair of transverse torsion tubes, each housing multi-leaf torsion bars rigidly located in the center, to which are attached a pair of trailing arms on each side. The trailing arms, in turn, support the stub-axle assembly by way of either king- and link-pins in pre-1966 models (prior to chassis number 116000001 in August 1965), or ball-joints on 1966-and-later Beetles. The reason for the use of multi-leaf torsion bars, consisting of a number of thin leaves, as opposed to one solid bar, is to ensure that the suspension doesn't end up being too stiff. As there is very little weight over the front wheels of a Beetle, too firm a torsion bar would result in an unacceptably hard ride.

Over the years, the number of torsion-leaves in each axle tube has been increased in an effort to make the suspension less harsh. To begin with, the earliest models came with four large leaves per tube, this increasing to four large leaves of softer rating,

supplemented by four small leaves. Later, with the advent of the new ball-joint suspension late in 1965, the number of small leaves was increased to six per tube, making a total of 10 torsion leaves. To damp the action of the torsion bars, a telescopic shock-absorber is fitted to each side of the suspension, while a hydraulic steering damper was added by the factory in 1960 in an effort to prevent front wheel 'shimmy' on rough surfaces.

At the back there are two separate torsion bars – solid ones this time – one for each side of the car. These have splines machined into them which locate in the chassis at the inner end and the trailing arms (spring plates) at the outer. There are 40 splines at the inner (chassis) end of each torsion bar and 44 at the outer (trailing arm) end. The reason behind the difference was so that small adjustments in ride height, and hence camber, could be made at the factory. By turning the torsion bar one spline at the inner end, the trailing arm would rotate 9°, while a one-spline change at the outer end would result in the trailing arm rotating by 8° 10′. Fine tuning can be achieved by rotating the torsion bar one spline at the inner end and then moving the trailing arm by one spline in the opposite direction – the net outcome will be a change in angle of just 50′, or slightly less than one degree.

All Beetles up until 1966 used this king- and link-pin design front suspension. The system works well as long as it is regularly maintained: it needs to be greased and adjusted periodically.

There were two rear suspension layouts used on the Beetle: swing-axle and IRS – or four-joint, as it is also referred to. The former was used throughout the Beetle's life and consisted of a pair of axle tubes, housing the drive shafts, which hinged at the inner (transmission) end and were bolted to trailing arms (more correctly termed 'spring plates') which were, in turn, connected to the torsion bars, as described earlier. The spring plates, while fulfilling the function of trailing arms, are designed to twist with the movement of the suspension. However, being made of spring steel, they try to resist this twisting motion, thereby aiding the torsion bars in their task of providing the springing element. The major drawback with this design is that any deflection of the suspension results in a change in camber at the back wheel, meaning the tyre no longer grips across the full width of its tread.

The IRS (short for 'independent rear suspension') design – a misleading term as it implies that the swing-axle system wasn't fully independent – was first seen on semi-automatic and US-specification models in the late-1960s. This featured four constant velocity (CV) joints, two on each side of the car, with an inter-connecting drive-shaft, and will be described in detail a little later.

Beetles built prior to 1960 were not equipped with any form of sway (anti-roll) bar, even though one was fitted to the contemporary Karmann Ghia models. In 1960, however, Volkswagen decided to install a sway bar to the front suspension of all Beetles in an effort to improve the handling characteristics. It has to be said, however, that the average driver would probably not have noticed much of an improvement in road manners.

For all the criticism the Beetle receives from non-believers, its handling characteristics are not as bad as they are made out to be. If that sounds like a case of damning it with faint praise, then maybe so, for there is definite room for improvement. In the early 1960s, American consumer vigilante, Ralph Nader, once he had finished getting his talons into the ill-fated Chevrolet Corvair, turned his attentions to the Volkswagen Beetle. Nader claimed that the car was inherently unsafe, citing that Beetles were unstable in a straight line, especially in cross-winds, and positively lethal round corners. For this, he blamed the swing-axle rear suspension, claiming that it was dangerous (the early Chevrolet Corvair was also a swing-axle design) and inevitably resulted in terminal oversteer when cornered hard.

The main fault with Nader's argument was that he ignored the fact that different cars require different driving styles. Because one car oversteers or understeers more than another doesn't make it any more or less dangerous than any other. At the time, most American-built cars had a heavy cast-iron engine mounted at the front, with a crude cart-spring live-axle arrangement at the rear. With an all-up weight of close to two tons, the average American sedan suffered dreadfully from understeer, especially on wet roads – all that weight over the front wheels meant that the car had a tendency to head straight on at corners. Nader, however, having been brought up on a diet of such vehicles, seemed reluctant to accept that understeer could be just as dangerous as oversteer.

In reality, the swing-axle Beetle can be driven hard and fast, even in stock form – after all, all road-going Porsches until the launch of the 911 had similar rear suspension and very few people ever criticised them for their handling. The required technique can be summed up in four words: slow in, fast out. Brake before you turn into a corner, progressively apply power as you negotiate the bend and accelerate hard out of it. Sure, if you get it all wrong – misread a bend, suffer a lapse of concentration – and decide to lift off the throttle half way round a long corner, the chances are that you will suffer what is called roll-oversteer: the shift in weight brought about by the change in speed will result in the outside rear wheel wanting to tuck under, causing the back of the car to jack itself up and lose grip. The result is the rapid onset of oversteer as the tail of the car wants to swap ends with the front. In most instances this can be corrected by swift application of opposite lock on the steering.

To call this characteristic dangerous is nonsense – it is rather like saying that the front brake on a pedal cycle is dangerous because, if you apply it too hard, you will be launched over the handlebars. You simply learn not to apply too much front brake pressure. Similarly, you need to appreciate that you should avoid lifting off the throttle mid-way through a bend when cornering hard in a Beetle.

Despite the best efforts of Ralph Nader to kill off the Beetle on the grounds of its handling characteristics, the car survived while Nader turned his attentions elsewhere. In August 1966, Volkswagen fitted an 'equalizer spring' (also known as a Z-bar) to the Beetle in an attempt to improve the handling characteristics.

The Z-bar arrangement was interesting in that it had no effect as a sway bar, serving only to stiffen the rear suspension on 'bump'. At the same time as the Z-bar was fitted, the torsion bars were made softer. Volkswagen issued a technical bulletin to its dealers explaining how the system worked:

'The main advantages of the equalizer spring in conjunction with softer springing are as follows:

1. The equalizer spring assists the rear torsion bars under load. On the one hand this permits a softer arrangement of the "main springing" and on the other hand the "main spring" and equalizer spring combine to give a progressive action. Consequently it was possible to adapt the suspension more efficiently to the individual load conditions. The softer torsion bars give a more comfortable ride because the equalizer spring only becomes active after a certain load.

2. Softer springing with one wheel under load because the force of the equalizer spring is only partially effective.

3. Due to the centrifugal forces acting on the body when cornering fast, the inner wheel is unloaded and the outer wheel loaded by the same amount. The equalizer spring does not become active at this stage. The tendency to more marked body roll, which results from softer torsion bars, forces the front axle, which is equipped with a stabilizer, to absorb additional cornering forces. The wheel load and lateral forces of the outer front wheel become proportionally larger. The transfer of wheel loads to the front results in neutral properties when the vehicle is cornering.'

The Z-bar certainly helped things but even so, one year later, the rear suspension was redesigned yet again on US-specification cars and European semi-automatic ('Stickshift') models, with the introduction of the new IRS system. This was later applied to the new 1302 Super Beetle range in August 1970 (followed by the 1303 series), resulting in a vast improvement in road holding.

The new rear suspension, which Volkswagen referred to as the 'Double Joint Axle', was described by the company as follows:

'This new design is a double-joint axle, with the rear wheels located independently on trailing and semi-trailing arms pivoting on the tubular frame cross-member. The trailing and semi-trailing arms, together with the cross-member, form a triangular swinging linkage which controls wheel

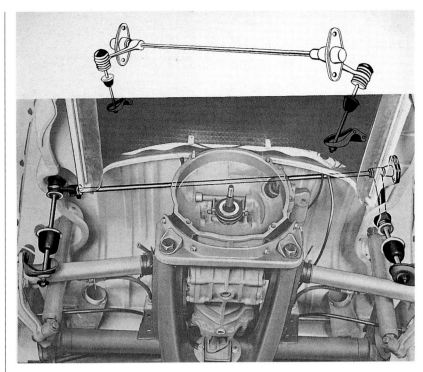

movement. Lateral forces at the rear wheels are transferred through the semi-trailing arms to the cross-member and thus to the frame. The half-shafts and final-drive do not therefore have to absorb any kind of thrust forces.

'The special advantages of this design lie in the very slight, but none the less intentional, alteration in the track and camber of the rear wheels over the whole extent of their travel. The camber of the rear axle, already slightly negative when the car is unladen, is increased slightly – as is the toe-in – over the suspension bump movement. Consequently, when cornering, load-transfer increases with increased loading for bump movement of the outside rear wheel. This results in uniform road-holding irrespective of the loading of the vehicle.'

The Super Beetles were also updated, although we hesitate to say 'improved', by the addition of MacPherson-strut front suspension in place of the former torsion bars. MacPherson struts are basically coil-over shock-absorbers which form one of the main structural elements of the suspension system (the others being the lower track-control arm and the radius rod – in the case of the 1302/3 models, the sway bar doubles as the radius rod, limiting any unwanted fore-aft suspension movement), with the top and bottom mounting points of the strut acting as the steering pivot points. The system was originally seen on the VW Type 4, launched in 1968, which was the first production Volkswagen to feature this front suspension design.

The MacPherson strut design was adopted by Volkswagen for two main reasons, one being that it allowed more efficient use to be made of the front luggage space – the spare wheel could be laid flat

The 1500 model, introduced in August 1966, saw a refinement of the swing-axle in the form of the addition of the 'equalizer spring', also known as a 'Z-bar'. This simple device helped to improve the Beetle's handling at speed.

Swing-axle design is very simple, with a pair of transverse torsion bars providing the springing. A pair of trailing arms (spring plates) connect to the axle tubes, which are designed to pivot at the inner, gearbox, end.

The IRS suspension is a better design altogether as far as handling is concerned. Although basically the same in layout as the swing-axle (it retains the torsion bars and spring plates), the IRS design does not use the axles as a structural element.

The main problem with the swing-axle design is that there is a considerable change in camber angle at the rear wheels when negotiating a bump, or rounding a corner. This can lead to some 'interesting' handling characteristics at speed!

The IRS design is far better in terms of handling, although there is still a small change in camber at the limits of suspension travel. For anyone searching for ultimate handling from their Beetle, starting with an IRS chassis may be the answer.

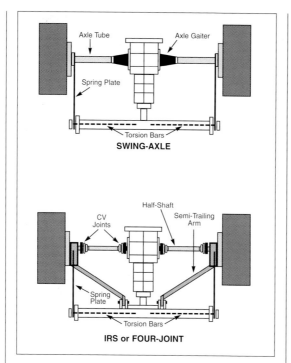

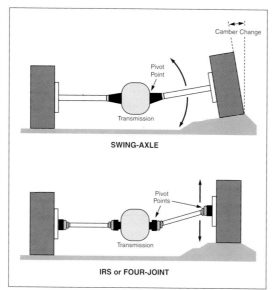

under the trunk floor and the luggage space made wider, the overall effect being to increase the carrying capacity by some 85%. The other reason for the change of design was to take advantage of the better handling characteristics offered by the MacPherson strut design. However, considering what an ill-handling, overweight car the Type 4 was, it is perhaps surprising that VW's engineers even considered copying its suspension set-up! Yet it has to be said that, when fresh out of the showroom, the 1302 and 1303 Beetles did appear to handle better than their predecessors. Note we say 'fresh out of the showroom' for, as soon as the rubber suspension bushes had started to wear, the strut inserts (the equivalent to the shock absorbers) had begun to lose their effectiveness and the springs had started to go soft, the result was a very poor-handling car indeed, with front end 'shimmy' being a common complaint from disgruntled owners.

For the ultimate in handling there is no substitute for a car with a four-joint IRS rear end, but opinions are divided on the merits or otherwise of the two alternative front end designs. To many, the 1968-on US-spec Beetles represent the ultimate, having the trusty torsion bar front end combined with the superior IRS rear. Others, especially those who indulge in circuit racing in the Super VW Cup (France) or Käfer Cup (Germany) championships, prefer the possibilities offered by the MacPherson strut design.

Thus far, we have only really considered the Beetle's suspension from the viewpoint of the person who wishes to corner hard, but suspension design also plays a very important part in the drag racer's life, even those who only take their car to the strip for the occasional trip down the quarter mile. For the most part, drag racers tend to use the potentially stronger swing-axle rear end, despite the fact that IRS offers superior traction on the startline. Why is this? Partly cost (beefing up the IRS drive-line is far more costly than modifying a swing-axle set-up) and partly blinkered tradition. Many race chassis builders openly acknowledge that IRS offers far more to the would-be drag racer, yet customer pressure dictates that the majority of race cars are built with swing-axle rear ends.

However, as we shall see, no matter what suspension design your Beetle came with, there are ways to improve matters, be it for Porsche-like cornering or better launches at the drag strip.

The Braking System
From rods and cables to front-wheel discs

The stock Beetle braking system has never been the most sophisticated or the most efficient ever devised, being best described as 'adequate' for the job in hand. The first Beetles – and indeed all standard models until 1962 – were fitted with mechanical drum brakes, operating on a system of rods and cables. The brakes were barely sufficient to cope with the stresses of a 25bhp engine and a 100km/h top speed and were prone to seizing solid in winter as the cables froze in their guides!

In March 1950, the factory began to install a hydraulic braking system on 'export' models (basically, the VW equivalent of a Deluxe Beetle) which was a distinct improvement but hardly anything to get excited about. In May that year, in an effort to improve the efficiency still further, the diameter of the master cylinder was reduced from 22.2mm to 19.5mm. The diameter of the rear brake cylinders remained 15.9mm until mid-1956 (with chassis number 1-397 022), after which the diameter was increased to 17.5mm. Then, in December 1953, VW moved the brake fluid reservoir from its hiding place on top of the master cylinder to a more accessible location behind the spare wheel.

Until August 1955 the emergency (parking) brake cables had always run right the way forward to the front of the car where they connected to a rod arrangement operated by the handbrake lever. This was a throwback to the days of the mechanical braking system in which, incidentally, the handbrake operated on all four wheels. After August, the handbrake cables were terminated at the lever itself, making life a lot easier for the DIY mechanic, as they could now be adjusted from inside the car, rather than having to lie under the front of the car and reach the cables through a tiny inspection panel. However, owners of the standard model had to make do with the old system.

In October 1957, the width of the front brake linings was increased from 30mm to 40mm and the diameter of the front wheel cylinders increased from 19.05mm to 22.2mm. The rear brake cylinders were increased from 17.5mm to 19.05mm at the same time. Along with these changes, new brake back plates were fitted, which allowed the front brake cylinders and adjusters to be mounted vertically. Aside from some detail modifications, the braking system remained largely unchanged until August 1966.

Prior to this point, to adjust the brakes, you had to remove the hubcap and insert a screwdriver, or similar implement, through an inspection hole in the brake drum itself. The new design dispensed with this hole on the drum, the adjusters now being accessible through a pair of holes on the brake backing plate. Another two holes allowed a visual inspection of the linings to be carried out.

Useful though this modification on the drum braking system proved to be, the big news for the 1967 model year was the introduction of front disc brakes on the 1500 sedans, with the exception of those destined for the USA. In fact, no Beetle would ever be exported to the United States with disc brakes fitted as standard – quite why this was so remains a mystery. The new disc brake assemblies were developed from those first seen on the Type 3 range in August 1965 and proved to be a major improvement over the old drum brakes. To complement this change, a new master cylinder was introduced.

As the disc brakes were of a far more compact design, the hub diameter was reduced, with the wheels now located by four bolts in place of the previous five. For a while, Volkswagen offered

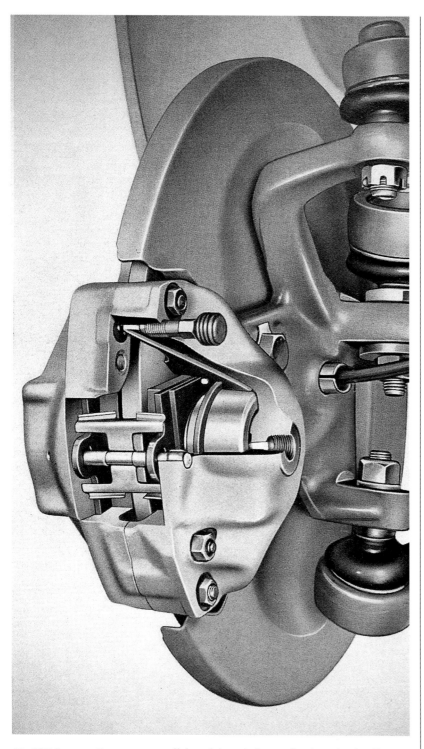

there would not be a total loss of braking, the front and rear brakes operating independently of each other. This system was initially introduced on the 1300 and 1500 models, but then found its way onto the 1200s in August 1969.

The dual-circuit braking system required the fitment of a new master cylinder, this being a tandem design, with the two separate brake pistons operating in line with one another. There were three separate outlets from the cylinder, a single one to the rear brakes and two individual outlets for the left and right front brakes. Later, in August 1970, with the introduction of the 1302 range, the master cylinder was redesigned, with just two outlets, the front brake pipe leading to a separate T-piece and then on to each front brake.

The only other changes made to the stock brake systems were alterations to the specification of the disc brake callipers when fitted, first to the 1302S and then to the 1303S models. A brake system warning light was also added for the 1969 models so the driver could carry out a quick check to see if the system was alive and well. It is interesting to note that the Beetle never benefited from servo-assistance and never saw the use of four-wheel discs, although both aftermarket servo and rear disc brake kits have been, or are, available.

Before You Start
Some suggestions before you start your new project

We have to make some assumptions before disturbing the beast which lies dormant within your Beetle. Assumption number one is that your engine is currently in fine health. By that we mean it has not covered an excessive mileage since its last rebuild (anything over 40,000 miles is quite enough, thank you) as any performance modifications, no matter how modest, are going to put more of a strain on it. In a stock motor, there is no reason why you shouldn't cover 100,000 miles without major overhaul, although there are some who will argue (the author included) that 60-65,000 miles is the practical limit before at least taking a look at the condition of the valve guides.

VW engines are prone to drop exhaust valves when high mileages have been covered and, as anyone who has experienced such a fate will tell you, it is not a pleasant experience. At best, you may get away with replacing a piston and having the cylinder head repaired (oh, and you'll need to change all the bearings, too, as the debris will have worked its way round the oiling system) but most likely the head will be history, the crankshaft journals scored, and parts of the damaged piston, which has been attacked by the valve, will have ended up in all kinds of expensive places. The author has seen otherwise good engines wrecked totally as a result of a dropped exhaust valve (it's

The VW disc assemblies were relatively unsophisticated, but got the job done. The design was first seen on the Type 3 models. For anyone with a later drum-braked Beetle, swapping to discs is definitely worthwhile.

parallel models with four or five-lug wheels, all 1500s having the four-lug type, the 1200 and 1300 sedans coming with the earlier style. It was not for another year that the four-bolt design would be adopted across the range, with the exception of certain base model 1200s.

In August 1967, the width of the rear brake shoes was increased from 30mm to 40mm and the diameter of the rear wheel cylinders changed to 17.46mm. However, the important news was the introduction of a dual-circuit braking system, the reservoir of which was relocated to the right side of the luggage compartment. The new system meant that, in the event of a leak in one of the brake pipes,

always the exhaust valve, and more than likely that of number three cylinder). Debris is created which gets wedged between a cam follower (lifter) and its bore with dire consequences for the case, cam and lifters alike.

Unless you know the history of the car in minute detail, then assume the worst and be prepared to overhaul the top end at the very least. By that we mean replacing the exhaust valves and their guides and checking the heads for cracks between the sparkplug holes and the valve seats. This, again, is a common failing with high-mileage VW engines, or ones which have been subjected to extreme heat. Type 2 engines are particularly vulnerable to this damage. Sure, the heads can be repaired but it may prove cheaper in the long run to buy replacements.

If the oil looks dark and sludgy, or the engine is very oily underneath, then be prepared to split the crankcase and check the condition of the crank and bearings. In fact, if you are going this far, replace the bearings even if the crank journals are OK. Why? That way you know they will be good for the next 100,000 miles, assuming you change the oil regularly. An oily underside to the engine suggests one of two things: the engine has been apart in the past and assembled by a ham-fisted mechanic who cares little for the finer points of VW engines, or it has covered a high mileage and has simply started to show its age. If the piston rings and cylinder bores are worn, then there will be excessive blow-by – that's when the combustion gases force their way past the piston rings and pressurize the crankcase, causing the oil within to look for the easiest point of exit from the engine! Usually this is from the crankcase breather but it can also be from around

the flywheel oil seal, the oil pump assembly, the pushrod tubes, the valve covers… Come to think of it, there is hardly a place where oil hasn't been known to leak from an old Beetle engine.

The second assumption we have to make is that you, as the car's owner, have some mechanical knowledge. If you don't already possess one, purchase a high-quality workshop manual for your car – the Bentley reprints of the original VW factory shop manuals are the best, but also the most expensive. However, as an old VW specialist used to say, buy the best and cry once. Once you've stopped crying, read the manual over and over again until you have familiarized yourself with the innermost workings of the engine.

As far as tools are concerned, you will at the very least need a range of both open-ended and ring-type wrenches, varying from 8mm up to 19mm in size. A good quality socket set covering at least that range will be invaluable, too, along with a selection of screwdrivers, a set of feeler gauges and a soft-faced hammer. If you plan on splitting the crankcase, or simply change the flywheel, you will also need to acquire a 36mm 3/4in-drive socket to remove the flywheel gland nut. You can also use this to remove the rear hub nut when you are carrying out brake or transmission repairs. The other items which you will need to carry out basic maintenance and make modest performance improvements will be a floor jack, axle stands and a torque wrench. Between them, these represent the largest areas of expenditure when equipping your home garage and you may feel you would rather borrow them from a friend. Well, that's fine but we guarantee that at some point in the future you'll wish you had your own.

A revelation came in the form of the 1967 1500 Beetle, which not only featured the new Z-bar rear suspension design, but also front disc brakes. The transformation was truly remarkable – the Beetle could at last stop safely from speed!

Mild Street

Building a Mild Street Engine
Suggestions on how to produce a reliable 60-65bhp

Add a set of aftermarket wheels, remove the chrome trim, install a lightly modified engine and you have the ideal recipe for low-cost fun in the form of a mild street Beetle. Such a car would make a perfect daily driver.

To briefly recap, the Beetle engine came in five different capacities: 1131cc, 1192cc, 1285cc, 1493cc and 1584cc. The first of these is the old 25-horse engine used in all VWs up until December 1953 (chassis no. 10 575 414), when it was superseded by the first of the 1192cc units, which produced a modest 30bhp (US 36hp). This engine is not to be confused with the later 1192cc 34bhp (US 40hp) engine used from chassis no. 3 192 507 in August

1960. In today's world, it is best to disregard the old 25- and 30-horse engines as far as performance modifications are concerned. They are an interesting part of Volkswagen history and there are indeed enthusiasts who advocate hot-rodding these old motors with period equipment from companies such as Okrasa and Denzel, ready to install them in their split- and oval-window sedans. As the author can vouch, an Okrasa-engined vintage Bug can be a

Swapping engines can be complicated by the variety of flywheels on offer over the years. Top left is the 109 tooth 180mm 6v; top right is the 130 tooth 180mm 12v; bottom left is the 130 tooth 200mm 12v; bottom right 130 tooth 210mm 12v used on the late Type 2. Beetles with 6v electrics used the 109 tooth flywheel, with the exception of the 1967 1500 model, which used the 130 tooth type with a special 6v starter motor. Late type flywheel may be installed on early crankshaft, but the early flywheel may not be used on later crank.

Even with a relatively modest 1641cc engine, this Beetle provides its owner with endless hours of fun on the street and strip. By keeping engine mods to a reasonable level, there is no reason why reliability should be compromised in any way.

lot of fun but it's no match for a Beetle with an up-to-date motor.

For many people, their first contact with the VW Beetle takes the form of a basic 1200 model with its 34bhp (US 40hp) 1192cc engine. This is indeed a worthy unit which will, figuratively speaking, last for ever. Regular maintenance in the form of frequent oil changes and valve clearance checks will see this engine cover a high mileage without any problems. However, with such a modest power output, the performance capabilities of any VW so equipped will fall far short of many people's expectations, especially if they have previously driven a more modern vehicle, such as a VW Golf.

Many times the question arises 'How can I improve the performance of my 1200 Beetle?' and the simple answer is, 'Do you think it's worth the effort?'. While it is perfectly possible to modify the engine and see a modest return for your efforts, in the long run it may make more sense to replace the engine with something like a stock 1600 dual-port unit – if you can find one. These engines are by far the most popular as far as swaps are concerned, so you may have to look around for a while to find a good one. Even then, unless you know its most intimate history, be prepared to carry out a routine strip and inspection of the top end.

Installing a late dual-port engine in any Bug which came with 12v electrics from the factory is quite simple, but you will have to make some changes if your car happens to be an earlier 6v model. The problem is that the flywheel fitted to

Installing an engine with a 12v 130 tooth flywheel in an early transmission will necessitate clearancing the bellhousing at the points shown here. Carry this out carefully using a die-grinder and remove as little material as possible.

To enable you to install a later 12v starter motor in the early 6v transmission, you will have to change the starter motor bushing to match the diameter of the new starter. Replacement bushes are available from most VW specialists.

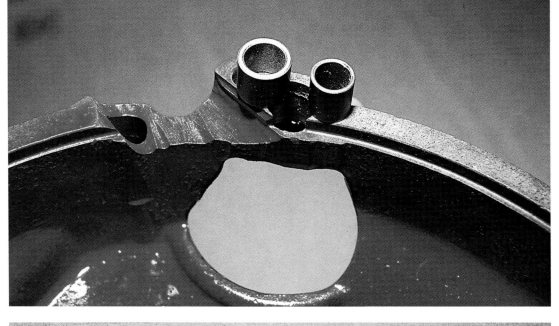

Two styles of clutch release assemblies were used. The top one was used up until 1971 and requires the use of a clutch pressure plate with thrust pad. Later type (bottom) may be installed in early transmission casing using the guide tube adaptor shown on left.

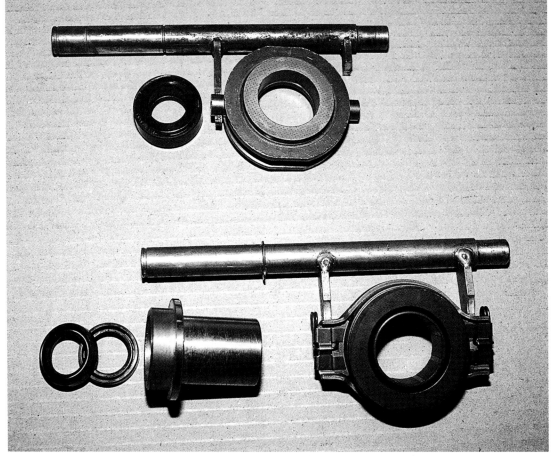

12v models had extra teeth on the ring gear (130 as opposed to the 6v flywheel's 109). It is also slightly larger in overall diameter, meaning that there can be clearance problems when using it in conjunction with an early-style transmission. There are ways round this, however. The starter motor can be changed for a 12v part as long as the bronze bushing in the transmission bell-housing is changed to suit, or you can fit the early flywheel to your later engine (but not, as it happens, vice-versa). If you opt for the later 12v 130-tooth flywheel, not only will you need the 12v starter, and hence have to convert the electrical system to 12 volts, but you will need to grind some material out of the early-type bell-housing to make room. The easiest way to do this is to offer the engine up to the transmission until it reaches the point where it will go no further. Turn the engine over with a socket so that the teeth of the flywheel mark the bell-housing. Then, with the engine removed once more, carefully grind out the

The best cooling system you can install is the factory so-called 'dog-house' fanshrouding and matching offset oil cooler. This is the largest cooler installed by VW on the Beetle and the offset design ensures uninterrupted airflow to all cylinders.

If you live in a cool climate, you can gain a few more horsepower by slowing down the cooling fan with the installation of a smaller 'power pulley'. However, these are not recommended for everyday use as the VW engine needs all the cooling it can get.

Early type release bearing was retained by two small hairpin clips. These are often troublesome and have been known to fall out, allowing the bearing to drop out of position. Always replace the clips whenever you install a new release bearing.

excess material with a die-grinder. Don't forget to wear a mask as the dust produced is very fine.

You will also need to pay attention to the clutch assembly – with the advent of the later IRS transmission (see section 2 for a description of the transmissions used by Volkswagen), the design of the clutch release mechanism changed to one where the release bearing moved back and forth along a guide tube; this precluded the use of the thrust ring on the clutch pressure plate. Fortunately, fitting a late engine in an early car only requires the use of an early-style clutch pressure plate, making that aspect of the conversion relatively simple.

One major problem with installing a late engine is that, as far as vehicles which originally came with a 25 or 30bhp (US 36hp) engine are concerned, the engine bay is far smaller, making the late engine –

especially a 1600 dual-port – a very tight fit indeed. Problems arise because the later engine is wider, as well as longer, than the earlier unit. This means you will experience difficulty while trying to install the rear engine tinware and also possibly run into problems with the rubber seal around the sides of the engine bay. A further obstacle is that the heat exchangers (heater boxes) will almost certainly foul the front of the engine bay at the bottom of the firewall. Volkswagen changed the angle of the

Several variations of the single-port cylinder head were used throughout the Beetle's life. Although it was a high-quality casting, the siamesed inlet port meant that there would always be a limit to the flow potential. Note extensive cooling fins.

The dual-port head was first seen on the Type 3 in 1968 and proved to be a hit among VW tuners from the word go. Its flow potential was vastly superior to that of even a modified single-port design, straight out of the box.

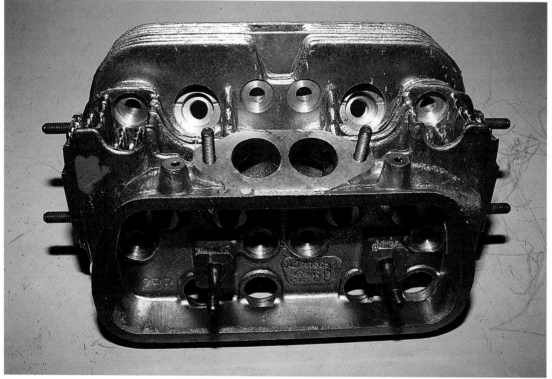

engine and transmission to cater for this in August 1960, by altering the design of the gearbox mountings at the same time as the later one-piece transmission was introduced.

Despite the minor problems which you may encounter, installing a later 1600 dual-port engine is certainly the easiest way to increase the performance of your 34bhp (US 40hp) 1200 Beetle, and it has the added advantage that you will be perfectly poised to further modify the engine at a later date, as finances allow. If a 1600 unit is not available, then you could always install a 1300 in either single- or dual-port form, or a 1500 engine. Any will be an improvement over the original and, in the case of a 1300 dual-port engine, this can easily be enlarged in capacity to match the power output of the 1600 unit.

If, however, there is a determination to retain the original 1200 engine, there are still some useful modifications which can be made.

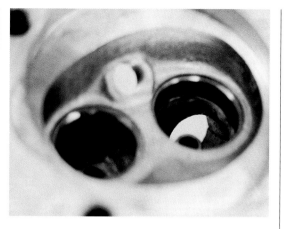

Looking down through the inlet port of this head, it is possible to see how restrictive the design is: very little of the inlet valve is visible. The boss protruding from the left side of the port is the valve guide, which also interrupts gas flow.

Even the dual-port head needs some help: the factory casting process is limited in what it can achieve in terms of port shape and finish. This area directly under the inlet valve seat needs to be radiused off for more efficient flow.

Viewed from the other (header) end, the restrictive design of the exhaust port can be seen clearly. Even if you do no other work to your heads, it would be worth carefully smoothing off the radius in the port.

The exhaust port on both single- and dual-port heads needs some real attention to allow the engine to breathe. There is a sharp radius below the valve seat which must be blended in smoothly. Take care not to undercut the valve seat itself.

This dual-port head is in the first stages of a mild porting job. Note how, even after a relatively small amount of effort, the port has been straightened and more of the valve exposed. Do not be tempted to remove the valve guide boss.

On the right is a stock dual-port head, while on the left is one which has been modified. Note how the combustion chamber has been opened up and the sharp edges blended. The head has also been fly-cut for increased compression.

Many years ago, the author modified the engine of his 1962 1200 sedan by porting the cylinder heads (principally by smoothing the sharp 90° bend in the exhaust port), raising the compression ratio slightly, replacing the carburettor with a progressive dual-choke Weber 28/36DCD and fitting an all-centrifugal advance distributor. The result was a basic Beetle which could accelerate from 0-60mph in just a little over half the time it took a stock 1200! The total cost amounted to very little, as the carburettor was sourced from a wrecking yard while the distributor was part of a swap with a friend. However, the only reason this route was taken was because, as a student, funds would not allow fitting a larger engine.

The next step up the ladder would have been to fit a 1340cc or a 1470cc conversion, both of which were popular at the time (early 1970s), followed by an extractor exhaust system. Today, these 'big-bore' conversions, which consisted of machined-down 1500 or 1600 cylinders fitted to the otherwise stock 1200 engine, are rare and frowned upon by most tuners as the cylinder walls were so thin, leading to distortion and consequent blow-by.

The principal way in which gains can be had from any VW engine is to improve its ability to breathe – by that we mean modifications to the induction and exhaust systems, as well as to the cylinder heads. The factory acknowledged this when it introduced the dual-port cylinder head. A stock 1200 or 1300 engine will benefit from fitting an extractor exhaust system of some description and there are several on the market, produced in a

variety of designs by such companies as Bugpack, S&S, Thunderbird, Scat and many others. A simple system with a single quiet-pack muffler will make a noticeable difference to the performance of a 1200 Beetle, although you shouldn't expect major increases in horsepower.

Changing the carburettor is the next worthwhile modification although, as far as the 1200 model is concerned, the choices are somewhat limited. At the time of writing, no-one offers an aftermarket carburettor kit for this engine although in the past there have been several different options available, including simple dual-carburettor conversions which allowed the owner to double-up on the stock Solex carb. Single carburettor conversions in the past included examples from Fish, Nikki and Holley although none were especially successful on this small engine. In real terms, there is little point in increasing the size of the carburettor unless the inlet manifold can be changed at the same time – the stock manifold is too small, as indeed are the inlet valves, to handle anything much larger than the regulation Solex 28PICT carburettor. Aftermarket manifolds are available to fit the single- and dual-port 1300-and-larger engines – usually as part of a complete kit – but not the 1200.

For mild street engines based in the 1300 and 1600 dual-port engines, the most popular single carburettor conversion is the 32/36DFEV Weber which is available from a variety of sources including Bugpack and Scat. These kits come complete with new inlet manifold center-sections,

An ideal carburettor set-up for the mild street engine is the well-proven dual Solex-Kadron system. This is probably the best budget induction system available for the Volkswagen engine and, with attention paid to jetting, works extremely well.

Smaller dual single-choke carburettors, be they Weber 34 ICTs or 'baby' Dell'Orto 36mm, are perfect for use on all engines up to 1600cc. Over that and you really need to use the 40mm Kadrons at the very least. Note quality aftermarket throttle linkage.

Replacing the stock Solex with a single Weber carburettor – in this case a 36DCNF – is a popular and effective conversion. Even with no internal modifications, just an aftermarket exhaust system and an-all centrifugal distributor, you will notice an improvement.

Believe it or not, this impressive-looking engine is actually just a 1300 fitted with dual Weber 34ICT carburettors. Although we're not keen on the aftermarket chrome fan-housing (it's not as efficient as a stock dog-house type), it shows what can be done.

which are designed to be used with the stock manifold end castings. Single-port engines can use these kits if the correct aftermarket end-pieces are fitted at the same time. In most cases, the carburettors come with jetting best suited to a stock 1600 and this may prove to be less than ideal if the kit is fitted to another engine. However, unless the carburettor is set up on a rolling road or an engine dynamometer, these conversions frequently result in a small flat-spot, or stumble, as the throttle is first opened. This is not a major fault but rather living proof that it is virtually impossible to offer a 'universal' carburettor kit which lives up to its name, so it's worth the time and expense involved in getting it set up properly. Bugpack, in fact, lists a set of jets for the Weber progressive carburettor to make this task easier.

On a 1600 dual-port engine, there are alternatives to the single progressive carburettor: dual 36mm single-choke Dell'Ortos, dual Weber 34ICTs or the popular dual 40mm Solex-Kadron carburettors. Any of these will offer a useful increase in performance without loss of economy or flexibility and have proved to be extremely popular among those on a strict budget.

If anything other than the stock carburettor and inlet manifold are used, then it is wise to change the distributor for one of all-centrifugal design. The stock distributors used on the majority of Beetle engines were of part-centrifugal, part-vacuum operation. By changing the breathing characteristics of the engine, the vacuum created in the inlet manifold will change, resulting in an alteration to the rate of ignition advance as the distributor will no longer respond as the factory intended. By swapping to an all-centrifugal distributor, such as a Bosch 009, 010 or an 050, this problem is cured as the rate of spark advance is purely dependent on engine rpm. At this level of tune, stock spark plugs are perfectly acceptable.

On a mild street engine – and by that we mean one which is expected to carry out regular daily-driver duties while providing a little extra performance for the minimum outlay – there are still some other avenues which are worth exploring. For example, the owners of 1300 dual-port engines might consider fitting a set of 1600 (85.5mm) cylinders and pistons which, with no other modification, will increase the capacity to 1584cc. Such conversions are available in two forms: bolt-on and machine fit. The former, as the name suggests, allows the owner to remove the existing 77mm cylinders and pistons and then replace them with the larger versions. Although the advantages are obvious, the disadvantage of this set-up is that the tops of the cylinders are rather thin and can result in poor sealing against the cylinder head, with a consequential loss of compression. Better are the machine-fit conversions which require the 1300 cylinder heads to be opened out to accept the stock-

A relatively modest engine can be made to feel more zesty by removing material from the rear of the stock flywheel. Taking the weight down to about 13lbs allows the engine to rev more quickly – any lighter and the smoothness suffers.

type 85.5mm cylinders. Owners of 1500 models (which have 83mm cylinders) can fit these 1600 conversions without any machining.

There is a bolt-on 88mm conversion available for the 1600 engine which increases the capacity to

Whenever you change the induction system on your engine, you will need to replace the original vacuum-advance distributor with an all-centrifugal type. This is the classic Bosch 010 unit – a better choice than the later replacement '009' in terms of quality.

1679cc without machining. However, this is not a recommended modification for the same reasons as cited earlier for the bolt-on 1300 to 1600 conversion. Once again, the better option is to choose the machine-fit conversion which requires the heads to be opened out to accept the new cylinders. This conversion can also be used with success on the 1300 engine, although the smaller valve sizes of the 1300 heads (33mm inlet x 30mm exhaust as opposed to the 1600's 35.5mm inlet x 32mm exhaust) will not allow the engine to breathe so efficiently. If the financial budget is tight, a bolt-on 87mm kit can be installed on a 1600 engine to give 1641cc – this is a popular and well-proven conversion which has proved to be reliable. Owners of 1300 engines will still need to have their cylinder heads machined to accept the larger cylinders.

For a daily-driver engine, we would not recommend that you change the camshaft, except for one of the very mild street cams on offer (such as Bugpack's 270° duration/0.396in lift cam), as the stock item allows excellent driveability throughout the rev range on an otherwise stock or mildly-modified engine. It is all too easy to render the car quite unpleasant to use around town by installing a high-lift, long-duration camshaft in an engine which is intended to be mild-mannered and reliable. A camshaft with a more radical profile will result in

a loss of bottom-end power and torque, the two things which you need most in a car which sees regular urban use. Increasing the cam duration (and, therefore, the length of time the valves are held open) will push the power output higher up the rpm range; radically increasing the valve lift will result in an increase in torque but only if other modifications (such as improving the cylinder heads, modifying the induction and exhaust systems or increasing the capacity) are carried out at the same time.

A mild increase in valve lift can be beneficial to an otherwise stock engine but this is perhaps best achieved by installing a set of 1.25:1 high-ratio rocker arms on the stock valve assemblies. Certainly this is far easier to carry out than changing the camshaft as there is no need to split the crankcase – all that is required is to remove the valve covers, the rocker assemblies and the stock rocker arms from the shafts. Replace these with the new high-ratio rocker arms and reassemble on the heads – preferably with a set of swivel-feet tappet screws to prevent the valve stems wearing prematurely.

To briefly recap: for the owner of a mild street VW designed to see regular daily use and who is working on a strict budget, we would recommend the 1200 or 1300 be swapped for a later 1600 dual-port engine. If further improvements are required, then consider changing the exhaust system first of all for an extractor system with either a single or a dual 'quiet' muffler (forget the noisy, inefficient glasspack type). This should then be followed by a change in the induction system courtesy of a single progressive carburettor conversion and matching manifold, along with the fitment of an all-centrifugal distributor. If an extra increase in power is required, a large-bore cylinder and piston conversion could be considered, along with a set of high-ratio rocker arms.

None of this work requires any major mechanical skills – indeed, much of it can be carried

A simple way to change the camshaft's characteristics is to install a set of 1.25:1 factory ratio rocker arms (left). These can be assembled onto stock valve gear and have the effect of increasing the valve lift. Stock rocker arm ratio is 1.1:1 (1.0:1 on 1200 models).

The stock exhaust system is extremely well designed but also extremely restrictive. Installing an aftermarket header system with even a single quiet-pack muffler will make a significant improvement. Avoid cheap systems with noisy glasspack mufflers.

A long time favourite among enthusiasts on a budget who wished to uprate the clutch of their early Beetle was a 9-spring 'Transporter' pressure plate. This unit was the most powerful offered by the factory in the days before aftermarket clutches.

Diaphragm clutches are available to suit early and late release bearings – 180mm unit on left is early type with thrust pad. 200mm pressure plate on right was installed in Beetles and Type 2s in the early 1970s. An excellent unit.

out with the engine still in the car. However, we must emphasize that the engine must be in sound condition before you start. If in doubt, check it out! For your efforts you could expect to see something in the region of 60-65bhp from a dual-port 1600 engine with a single dual-choke carburettor (or a pair of small single-chokes), a quality extractor exhaust and a set of ratio rockers. OK, so it's not ground-shaking, but you will certainly feel the difference if you've been used to a stock 1200 – after all, it will produce almost double the horsepower!

TRANSMISSIONS FOR MILD STREET USE
How to get the best from what the factory has to offer

For the person who is running a modestly-tuned engine in their Beetle, there really is not too much to be gained from carrying out transmission modifications, other than to fit a late gearbox into an earlier car, as outlined in the introductory chapter, so as to benefit from synchromesh on all four gears. One good reason to make a gearbox change at this level is to take advantage of a 'box with a higher final drive ratio, in order to give better fuel economy. The higher the final drive ratio (or the lower the numerical figure, for a 3.78:1 ring and pinion is considered to be a higher ratio than a 4.375:1), the lower the engine rpm will be for a given road speed. As long as the engine is capable of turning the higher gears, you will theoretically see an increase in fuel economy. A stock 1200 engine may struggle to cope with a 3.875:1 final drive, for example, whereas a mildly tuned 1600 which is used for regular freeway driving would positively benefit from such a swap.

As an example, when cruising at 70mph, the engine of a Beetle with a stock 1200 transmission and running tyres which are 24.5 inches tall, will be turning at 3738rpm. Switch to a transmission with a 3.875:1 final drive and the engine speed falls to 3310rpm. It may not sound much, but a 400rpm decrease will make a significant difference to the fuel economy.

As far as the clutch is concerned, installing a heavy-duty, factory-style pressure plate is one way to beef up your 180mm clutch, but the simplest way to ensure you have no slippage problems is to use a 200mm clutch and flywheel assembly from a 1500 or 1600cc Beetle. The late 200mm diaphragm clutches are very strong and can happily handle up to 100bhp without too much problem. When installing an uprated clutch pressure plate, check that you have the correct type: pre-1971 models used a different release bearing to the later ones, which required a thrust pad on the pressure plate. An early-style pressure plate (with pad) can be used with a later transmission by simply removing the thrust pad.

As the stock VW transmission has been known to survive the rigours of 120+bhp abuse (although this is definitely not recommended!), it is fairly unlikely that you will experience any failure as the result of running a 65bhp 1641cc engine combination, or similar. However, having said that, if you are in the regular habit of side-stepping the clutch away from road junctions, or trying your hand at the local drag strip, the chances are that you may indeed succeed in breaking something. In the first instance, you will probably end up breaking the differential, while in the second, you may break an axle, if you are extremely unlucky. For the most part, though, as long as your transmission mountings are in good order and you don't behave like a man or woman possessed every time you get behind the wheel of your Beetle, you should be safe in the knowledge that the Volkswagen engineers did their homework all those years ago. Without a doubt, the VW transmission is a real gem, a fact that did not escape Hewland, the famous racing transmission specialists, who based their original race transaxle on the humble Volkswagen unit.

SUSPENSION IMPROVEMENTS
Mild modifications can make all the difference.

In similar fashion to the transmission, it could be argued that, as long as the stock suspension is in perfect shape, you need not be concerned about making too many changes to the factory specification. However, there are considerable benefits to be gained from making sure that the suspension is exactly as the factory intended. In addition, a simple change of shock-absorber, or decambering the back end of a swing-axle model, can make a big difference to the way your Beetle handles.

Taking a look at the front end first of all, you should ensure that on pre-1966 models the king- and link-pin assemblies, or the ball-joints on later cars, are in good order. Although there are provisions for slight adjustment for wear on the link-pin assemblies, there is no way to adjust the king-pins or later ball-joints. Once worn, they must be replaced. In addition to this, you need to check the bearings which locate the trailing arms in the torsion tubes. This can be done with the car jacked up – any movement which can be detected between the trailing arm and the torsion tube will suggest the need to replace the bearings. While you're under the car, have a look at the anti-roll bar mountings. These frequently rust, allowing the bar to drop onto the road. Replace the mounting clamps and rubber bushes at the first signs of deterioration.

Check also the condition of the shock absorbers and steering damper: if either have lost their efficiency, or are leaking, they must be replaced. The steering box itself may also be worn – this can be checked by lightly rocking the steering wheel from side to side with the car at rest. The rim of the wheel should not move by more than about 1-2ins before resistance is felt. Some adjustment can be made to the steering box, but care must be taken not to adjust it so that the steering becomes stiff as

Two basic types of clutch are available, the one on the left being a diaphragm unit, that on the right using coil springs. In general, early 6v models used coil spring type, later 12v cars the diaphragm style. The unit shown is early type with release arms.

When installing a clutch with release arms, make sure you remove the clips which are installed by the manufacturer to preload the assembly to aid installation. Failure to do so will result in possible damage to the clutch unit.

Beetles built from August 1965 need to have particular attention paid to the condition of the ball-joints. Inspect the rubber boots for splits and check for excessive play: worn ball-joints result in poor handling. Mark on ball-joint should always face to front of car.

You should also check the condition of the bearings in the ends of the torsion bar tubes on the front axle beam. This holds true whether your car has ball-joint or earlier king- and link-pin suspension. Replacement requires removal of trailing arms.

the wheels are turned. If it is not possible to make the necessary adjustment without this happening, the steering box needs to be replaced or overhauled.

At the back end of your Beetle, check the shock absorbers and the condition of the rubber bushes which locate the trailing arms and the outer end of the torsion bars. This is best achieved by removing the four bolts which hold the torsion bar cover in place to expose the outer rubber bush. If this is badly distorted, the chances are the inner bush (located

behind the trailing arm) will also be damaged. If this is the case, these will need to be replaced. On IRS Beetles, in addition to the above check, you will also need to ascertain that the bushes at the inner ends of the semi-trailing arms are in good order. If not, the toe-in setting will vary dramatically with suspension movement, making the car feel very 'nervous' on corners.

Finally, you should check the condition of the front and rear wheel bearings. To check the fronts, jack the car up and grasp the top and bottom of the front tyre and try to move it back and forth. Repeat the procedure grasping the tyre at the 9 o'clock and 3 o'clock positions. If you can detect any movement, then the bearings will need adjustment or replacement. Once you have adjusted the bearing free-play, spin the wheel and feel for any roughness which will indicate excessive wear on the bearing races. If this is the case, replace the bearings. At the rear, jack the car up and, with the parking brake off, try to move the wheel up and down and side to side. You should not be able to detect any movement at all. If you do, once again the bearings will need to be changed for new ones.

Owners of 1302 and 1303 models will need to carry out some quite different checks of their own regarding the front suspension of their Beetle. The MacPherson strut arrangement relies heavily on the condition of rubber bushes which locate the inner ends of the track control arms and the sway bar, the latter doubling as a radius rod. With even just slight deterioration of the bushes, the suspension components are allowed to move in ways which the original engineers never intended. The end result is a constant 'shimmy' through the front wheels which feels initially like badly out of balance wheels. It is

possible to drive through this vibration, but it never goes away.

This malaise is a common failing on Super Beetles and one for which there is no cure other than to systematically replace each component as it shows signs of wear. In addition to worn rubber bushes, weak or leaking strut inserts, worn upper strut bearings and worn lower ball-joints can all be contributory causes to this problem.

Once the suspension has been thoroughly overhauled and returned to original condition, the chances are that you will notice quite a considerable improvement in the way your Beetle handles. If you wish to take things a stage further, then the first step should be to replace the standard shock absorbers with a set of uprated units from a company such as Koni, Bilstein, Spax or KYB.

Konis are generally regarded as being the best, as they can be rebuilt at a later date should they show signs of wear. They are adjustable for rebound damping, this being achieved by removing the unit from the car, compressing it fully and then turning the bottom half clockwise in relation to the top, as viewed from below. Spax units can be adjusted on the car with a screwdriver – there is a small adjusting screw on the side of the damper. KYB are

If you own a 1302/1303 'Super Beetle' you should invest in a pair of coil spring compressors (right) to allow you to remove the road spring so that the strut inserts (damper units) can be removed and replaced when they show signs of wear.

One of the best – and simplest – ways to improve handling is to install a set of quality uprated shock absorbers. These adjustable Koni units (far right) are among the best, with the advantage that they can be rebuilt. If you cannot afford a full set, install them at the rear.

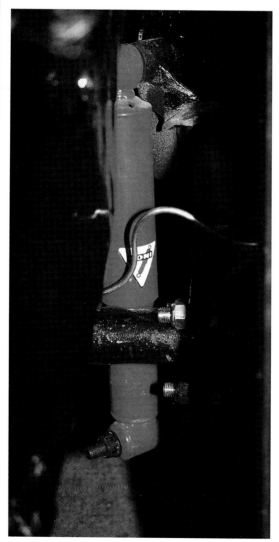

All 1200 and 1300 Beetles left the factory with drum brakes on all four wheels. Owners of ball-joint models can uprate the front brakes to discs by purchasing a kit like this, consisting of new spindles, discs, callipers, bearings and mounting bolts.

low-cost, non-adjustable units which are readily available from many specialists and, while not offering the versatility of the more costly Koni or Spax shock absorbers, will make a definite improvement to the handling characteristics of your car when fitted all round, making the suspension feel firmer and the car less prone to pitch and roll on corners.

In many ways, this is probably about as far as you need to proceed with a mildly-tuned street car. Sure, if you own a pre-1960 model, installing a standard sway bar would make a difference (they had been fitted as standard to Karmann Ghias but somehow the Beetle slipped through the net!) and decambering the rear suspension would help even further. However, we shall deal in more detail with suspension lowering in the subsequent section on building a fast road Beetle.

UPRATING THE BRAKING SYSTEM
How to get the best from your Beetle using factory parts

While the stock brakes on a Beetle are not exactly the latest in high technology, with even the disc brakes fitted to certain '67 and later models hardly inspiring great confidence, it has to be argued that they are adequate for their intended purpose. Just that: adequate. Their intended purpose was, when you think about it, to slow a relatively light sedan from 100km/h, or thereabouts, to rest on roads which were not exactly heaving with traffic. It didn't matter too much in the late 1940s and early '50s that your Beetle couldn't 'stop on a dime and have ten cents change', as the saying goes. However, as traffic increased and Beetles got faster (in relative terms!), it became obvious that something was going to have to happen in the braking department.

The first real move in this direction came when VW installed disc brakes on the 1500 Beetle in August 1966, although it has to be said that these weren't the greatest disc brakes ever designed, offering little more in braking effort than a well-maintained set of drums. Where the discs did score, though, was in their resistance to fade when braking from speed, or after repeated attempts to stop. Anyone who has driven down a steep mountain road in an early Beetle will need no reminding of the drum brakes' characteristic loss of efficiency when they get hot. Eventually things appear to get

Installation of the disc brakes begins with the removal of the stock drums and their spindles. To do this, you must undo the ball-joint assemblies, which will require the use of a special tool available from regular tool suppliers.

The new spindles – which incorporate the mountings for the brake callipers – are simply installed in place of the originals. Now would be a good time to ensure the ball-joints and brake hoses are in good condition. Replace them if there is any doubt.

so bad that pushing the brake pedal has little or no effect at all.

For anyone who has carried out some mild engine mods to his or her Beetle, the most obvious upgrade is to install a set of factory disc brakes at the front – that's assuming they haven't already been installed. The problem here is that disc brakes can only be fitted to ball-joint Beetles (that means, ones built after August '65), owners of earlier link-pin models being somewhat left out in the cold in this respect. However, as we are only dealing with power outputs in the region of 60-65bhp or so, a well-maintained set of factory drum brakes should be up to the task of providing the necessary retardation. Make sure you check right through the whole system, replacing suspect master cylinder, wheel cylinders, linings, pipes and hoses.

Owners of early 1950s Beetles can upgrade their braking systems to the mid-1960s specification simply by exchanging the drums, backing plates, wheel cylinders and master cylinder with those of the later type. Although this won't make your car stand on its nose, it will at least enable you to benefit from 10 more years of factory development!

One of the simpler modifications to make is to install the rear brake assemblies from an early Type 3, which increase the friction area from 258sq cm to 445sq cm – a hefty 72% increase. This will help, but does not totally transform the Beetle's stopping abilities into those of a Porsche (a marque whose name will reappear later in connection with hot road-legal VWs).

So, as far as making a modest improvement to the brakes of your Beetle, owners of king-pin models

Install new wheel bearings in the combined brake disc/hub using a suitably-sized drift, then pack the bearings with grease before offering the disc up to the stub axle. Now all you need to do is fit the outer bearings and spindle clamp.

The new calliper is located on the spindle by two high-tensile bolts, which should be torqued up to 42lbft (6kgm). Make sure you install locking tabs on each bolt before you tighten it up. In theory, bolts should not be reused.

should upgrade their front drum brakes to the most modern specification available (basically, that means 1965 spec) and install early Type 3 brakes at the rear. Owners of ball-joint models should install the factory disc brake set-up at the front (if not already fitted) and, once again, use Type 3 rear drums. It goes without saying that the rest of the system should be checked thoroughly. Incidentally, when the factory introduced the disc brakes late in 1966, the master cylinder was changed in design to incorporate a check valve (or residual pressure valve) which helped to maintain pressure in the

brake lines. Ideally, when installing disc brakes in place of drums, you should change the master cylinder accordingly. However, it is now extremely difficult to obtain the correct type as only one model is now listed. In practice, you should feel no difference between the two types of cylinder and need not be too concerned about this aspect of the conversion.

By the end of this chapter, we should now have a Beetle which produces around 60-65bhp (meaning that its performance will be greatly improved), has a reliable transmission, handles at least as well as the factory intended – if not better – and stops without too much drama. In fact, a car which will serve you well as a daily-driver for many years to come (or at least, until the desire to go even faster becomes too strong to resist!).

All that remains to be done is to install the brake hoses and refill the brake fluid reservoir with fresh hydraulic fluid. Bleed the brakes thoroughly and be prepared to enjoy the sensation of your Beetle's new-found braking efficiency!

Fast Road

FAST ROAD ENGINES
In search of a reliable 120bhp

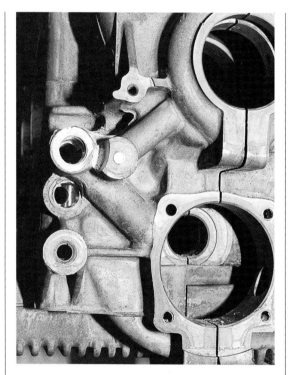

It is vital to pay particular attention to the oiling system of any high-performance Volkswagen engine. You should have the main oil galleries drilled and tapped, not only to allow a full-flow system to be used, but also to enable you to clean the case thoroughly.

The next step up the ladder from mild street tuning will require considerably more expenditure and effort, but the end results will certainly be worth it. Once again, there have to be certain assumptions made, one of which is that the base engine will be a late-model dual-port unit, ideally a 1600 to take advantage of the more efficient cylinder head design (larger valves and ports) and improved crankcase. Anyone with a 1200 or early 1300/1500 engine would be best advised to find a later engine before considering building a fast road engine.

Now, what do we mean by a 'fast road' engine? Well, we would envisage such a unit to be capable of reliably producing something in the region of 100-120bhp, but to do so will require the use of many aftermarket components, an increase in cubic capacity and either extensive reworking of the stock cylinder heads, or the use of aftermarket castings. The cost of such an engine, while not matching that of an all-out 180bhp large-capacity motor, will necessarily be considerably more than that of a mild daily-driver engine.

The base of any good high-performance engine should be a late-model dual-relief valve crankcase, as used on the dual-port 1300 and 1600 engines. These cases are easily identified by the two separate oil-pressure valves, one being located under the case adjacent to the flywheel, the other next to the oil pump. Earlier 1300 and 1500 single-relief valve cases are good castings but, where there is a choice, always opt for the later type as it offers a better lubrication system. If you are looking at a possible donor engine which is still fitted into a car, look for engine numbers which begin with one of the following code letters: B, C, AB, AC, AD, AE, AF, AG, AH, AJ, AK, AL, AR or AS.

While on the subject of crankcase code letters, there has always been much debate over the merits, or otherwise, of certain materials used in the casting process. Gene Berg Enterprises in the USA maintain that those cases marked with the casting code 'AS21' are far stronger than those marked 'AS41'. This code can be found either along the side of the sump or adjacent to the flywheel. While the AS21 cases are almost certainly superior to the AS41 type, there need not be too much concern about long-term reliability as both types have been used with success for many years in all kinds of applications.

One modification to the stock case which you will have to have done is to drill and tap it for a full-

Don't forget to drill and tap the opposite end of the oil galleries, behind the flywheel. These can then be plugged with a threaded pipe plug which may be removed at a later date to allow the oilways to be cleaned.

You should use a good quality oil pump cover – the range offered by Gene Berg Enterprises is among the best. Avoid using a cast aluminium cover as these are prone to wear, resulting in lost oil pressure.

is the life-blood of any engine and it pays to take steps to keep it clean. Use a high-quality filter – the HP1 model from Fram is the industry favourite – and remember to replace it each time you change the oil. On the matter of oil pumps, a good quality 'blue-printed' stock pump, such as that offered by Gene Berg Enterprises, or an aftermarket Melling cast-iron pump, which has larger gears for more volume, will be ideal. Use a Berg cast-iron cover plate – they are excellent quality and rarely leak if installed correctly - to allow the oil to pass out of the pump into the external oil lines. If you are concerned about excessively high oil pressure on start-up, use one of Berg's covers with a built-in pressure relief valve.

As for cooling, use the stock late-model 'dog-house' cooler and matching fan-shrouding. This will be more than adequate for most applications, although you should always run an oil temperature gauge as an added safeguard so that you can monitor what is happening. Keep the oil temperature below 100°C (212°F) where possible. If you do many long journeys on the freeway in a hot climate, you could consider adding an extra oil cooler in the oil lines which run to your new remote filter. An in-line thermostat will prevent the oil from running too cool when the ambient temperature falls by shutting off the oil flow to the cooler. As for where to mount the extra cooler, there are several possibilities, one being under the rear wheel arch (protected by a stone-guard) or alongside the transmission, with a duct to channel air into the cooler. The final improvement you need to make to the oil system is to install a deep sump – 1.5qt extension is perfect for a road car, virtually doubling the stock oil capacity (when used with an external oil filter etc) without undue loss of ground clearance. Consider a

flow oiling system. This requires the lower main oil gallery (on the left side of the engine as viewed from the rear of the car) to be drilled out and a ³/₈ NPT thread cut to allow an oil line fitting to be installed. This needs to be carried out professionally, and afterwards you must ensure that every last fragment of swarf has been cleaned out of the oilways and from inside the crankcase. The outlet side of the oil pump also needs to be blocked off (preferably with a threaded pipe plug) and an oil-pump take-off cover installed to allow the oil to pass from the pump out into external oil lines to a remote 'spin-on' filter and then back into the case at the main oil gallery. The reason this needs to be carried out is that the stock oil filtering system is woefully inadequate, consisting of nothing more than a crude gauze filter in the sump. While this may be (just) acceptable for a stock engine, it is certainly nothing like adequate as far as a high-performance engine is concerned. Oil

A fine example of a well-presented engine in a fast road VW. Bosch 009 distributor is used, along with dual Dell'Orto 40DRLA carburettors. Note use of power pulley and block-off plate over original fuel pump mounting (an electric pump is used).

The simplest way to increase the engine capacity is a big-bore conversion, such as this 90.5mm (1776cc) kit. Many people prefer this bore size over the larger 92mm (1835cc) conversion as they feel it is less prone to cylinder blow-by.

The CIMA/Mahle conversions use high-quality forged pistons which come from the factory with a graphite coating to help retain oil and reduce friction. Bolt-on conversions are available to give 1641cc and 1679cc, although the latter is not recommended.

deep sump a necessity on any modified VW engine.

If the crankcase you have chosen has been used in the past, there are some checks you need to carry out. Take a look at the main bearing saddles. Can you feel a ridge where the bearing shell has pounded its way into the case? This will probably have been caused as a result of the engine having covered a high mileage. You should get the case checked out by a specialist machine shop and be prepared to have it align-bored – this is the process whereby the main bearing saddles are machined to accept an 'oversized' bearing (not to be confused with an 'undersized' bearing, which is used in conjunction with a reground crankshaft). This machine process removes the wear and tear and ensures that the bearings are perfectly aligned in the crankcase. Some people frown upon this process, claiming that the VW case was never meant to be rebuilt, but many such cases have been put to good use over the years, even in high-horsepower race motors.

Another check is to see if there are any cracks behind the flywheel. It is not at all uncommon to find a crack adjacent to number 3 cylinder, especially if the case has previously been bored for oversize cylinders and pistons. Cracked cases can be repaired but if you are planning on building your new engine from scratch, it would be better to pass such a case by and find a better example. Look, also, for signs of the cylinder heads studs having pulled from the case – over-tightening or excessive cylinder temperatures could have caused the studs

to have pulled out of the case. Again, this is not necessarily a catastrophic state of affairs but it does make more sense to find a good case in the first place.

Early cases had 10mm studs which screwed directly into the alloy casting, while later ones, produced from September 1972 onwards, came with steel inserts designed to take 8mm studs. This all but cured the problem, once and for all, although it is possible to fit larger threaded inserts in the late-type case which accept the old-style 10mm studs, the consensus being that they are stronger than the thinner 8mm studs.

Aside from these checks, take a good look at the case in general and search for signs of accident damage or general maltreatment. Are the mounting lugs for the oil-cooler intact? Have the oil pump studs been over-tightened? Have the holes which accept the main bearing dowels become elongated? Is the case badly corroded? Are the lifter (cam follower) bores intact, or are there signs of lifters having seized in the case? As the case is the foundation on which your new engine is to be built, it pays to spend a little time reassuring yourself you have made the right choice.

In the search for a reliable 100-120bhp engine, it is possible to take a number of different routes, each of which will have merits and disadvantages. Starting at the bottom, so to speak, the simplest way to achieve an immediate gain in horsepower is to increase the capacity of the engine to either 1776cc,

1835cc or 1914cc. Each of these conversions allows the stock 69mm crankshaft to be used, the late 'F-type' cross-drilled crank used from 1968 onwards being a particularly fine component. However, better still would be such a crank which has been counterweighted – ie, had counterweights welded in place on the webs which help to improve the balance of the crank at higher rpm. If you do not envisage your engine seeing more than 5,500rpm then a counterweighted crank may be something of a luxury, but as we are expecting 'our' engine to see some serious use on the street, and maybe the strip on occasion, then counterweighting is highly recommended. Such cranks are available outright from a number of sources, or you can approach a company like Rimco in the USA to have your own crank modified.

In addition to counterweighting, another necessity as far as a fast road engine is concerned is to have the crank and flywheel assembly 8-dowelled to prevent the two parting company. In stock form, the flywheel is located on the crank by just four small hardened steel dowels and a large 36mm gland nut. This is fine for a daily driver, but start to put your car to more serious use and the chances are good that the flywheel will eventually come loose, damaging itself and the end of the crankshaft in the process. To prevent this from happening, have a machine shop drill the crank and flywheel for an extra set of dowels (most aftermarket counterweighted cranks will already have been so

A classic California Look sedan: replica BRM wheels, nose-down 'hot-rod' stance and a hot engine give Frenchy DeHoux's '67 a certain style which can be achieved only with careful planning, patience and plenty of attention to detail.

modified) and then use a heavy-duty gland nut with at least a 1.5in head. Tighten this to around 300lb ft of torque (the stock gland nut takes 217lb ft) and the assembly should be capable of handling most of the abuse you are likely to throw at it. As for the flywheel itself, on any tuned engine – and any stocker over 1500cc – then it is imperative you use the later 200mm type (a reference to the diameter of the clutch friction surface).

The 1776cc (90.5mm bore), 1835cc (92mm) and 1914cc (94mm) conversions will need to have the crankcase machined to accept the larger cylinders and pistons. If the case is machined for

90.5mm cylinders, it will also accept the 92mm conversion, which uses cylinders of the same outside diameter, meaning that the cylinder walls of the latter will be thinner and possibly more prone to distortion. The larger 94mm conversion calls for the case to be opened up more. In each instance, if the stock cylinder heads are to be used in one form or another, they will also have to be machined to

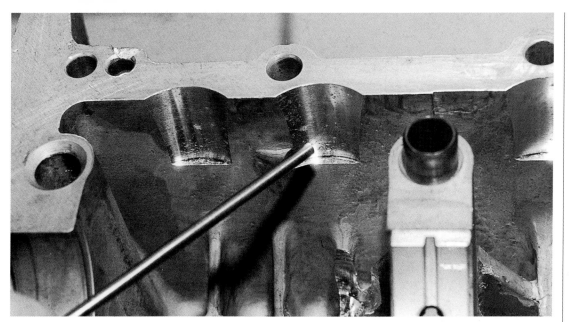

With strokes of 78mm and above, notably when using stock type rods, the case needs to be opened up at the top to allow adequate clearance. A shop like Rimco will have the necessary equipment to carry out this work quickly and accurately.

accept the new cylinders – there is no such thing as a 'bolt-on' 1776, 1835 or 1914cc conversion.

While a well-built large-bore, stock-stroke motor can be made to reliably produce our target power output, there really is no substitute for extra cubic inches in the form of including a long-stroke crankshaft in the parts list. Such cranks are available off the shelf in several different forms (see the relevant chapter in the sister publication *Aircooled VW Engine Interchange Manual* for a complete listing) but for a fast road engine we would recommend a good quality one-piece forged 78mm crank from a reputable company such as Bugpack, Scat or Gene Berg Enterprises. Each of these cranks is a new forging, as opposed to a welded and restroked stock crank, meaning that it is stronger and will last longer. Each comes ready drilled to accept an 8-dowelled flywheel.

With a set of 90.5mm cylinders and pistons, a 78mm crank will result in an engine of 2007cc, while 92mm cylinders give 2074cc and 94mm cylinders, 2165cc. The beauty of a 78mm crankshaft is that it will require very little clearancing inside the stock crankcase, even when used with bulky stock-type con-rods, although you will need to fit spacers under the cylinders to take into account the greater throw of the crankshaft. Longer stroke cranks, such as an 84mm stroker, while certainly helping to create a larger capacity – and, potentially, more powerful – engine add considerably to the cost and workload on the part of the builder. In addition they will require the use of special 'stroker' pistons, which have a shorter compression height than a stock piston so that they do not protrude from the end of the cylinder at the top of the stroke. Spacers placed under the cylinders allow you to make fine adjustments to compensate for the increased stroke.

To fit within a stock crankcase, these longer-stroke cranks also call for the use of more compact aftermarket con-rods with smaller rod journals –

Any performance engine must have the crank and flywheel drilled for four extra retaining dowels. That way, you virtually eliminate any possibility of the flywheel coming loose on the crankshaft – a trick discovered by Porsche in the 1950s.

If you are using a stroker crankshaft, you will almost certainly need to install spacers under the cylinders to allow for the increased piston travel. These spacers are available in a variety of thicknesses to allow fine adjustment of cylinder deck height.

A Cabriolet makes a great fast road car! With its lowered suspension and a warm 1776cc engine, Wayne Elam's example looks great beneath the cloudless Arizona sky. Polished EMPI-style 5-spoke wheels look particularly attractive.

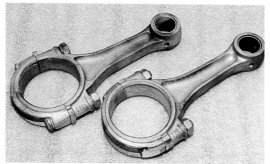

Fast road engines which use cranks with a stroke no greater than 78mm can happily use a modified factory rod, such as the Rimco Super Rod shown here on the right. Clearanced for extra stroke and with stronger bolts, it is an excellent choice.

typically 53mm Porsche as opposed to the stock 55mm Volkswagen. For an ultimate street engine this is obviously the route to take, as the higher the horsepower demands, the less suitable a factory-style rod becomes, quite apart from there being no substitute for the increase in capacity gained from installing a longer stroke crankshaft. However, for a reliable fast road combination, a 78mm crank with factory-style rods is perfectly adequate.

A stock '311' (a reference to the later part number) VW con-rod is fine for mild road use with anything up to a 78mm stroker crank, but making

greater demands than this can lead to failure of the rod bolts at high rpm. Companies such as Rimco replace the stock rod bolts with high-quality SPS-type components, machine the side of the rod for extra crankcase clearance and then balance and shot-peen the finished item for longevity. These so-called 'Super Rods' are a popular choice among budget-minded engine builders as they offer excellent value for money, combined with greater strength.

Moving onto the cylinder heads themselves, any appreciable increase in cubic capacity is going to require an increase in valve size to allow the engine to breathe properly. While a mild 1776cc unit with a single carburettor will perform quite satisfactorily with the stock 35.5mm x 32mm valves, a 78mm x 94mm fast road engine with dual Webers would certainly feel strangled. For any engine of 1776cc and over which runs dual carburettors and a high-lift, long-duration camshaft, it is vital that the valve sizes be increased to at least 40mm inlet and 35.5mm exhaust. Once the engine size exceeds 2 litres, then there is a strong argument for going up to 42mm inlet valves with 37mm exhausts, especially if outright performance is a prime concern.

The factory dual-port casting is a good starting point for producing an efficient large-valve head for

When assembling your new engine, always build it up in the left half of the crankcase. Note how much space the counterweighted stroker crank takes up inside the case. Don't forget to install the O-rings round the main bearing studs.

use on a fast road engine and is probably better than some of the less expensive aftermarket items, such as the so-called '041' head. The latter is a dual-port casting produced in South America, which comes with 39mm inlet and 32mm exhaust valves. Although the inlet valve size may be larger, the actual inlet port is little different to that of the stock head, hence gas-flow through the port is little better than if the original head had been retained. In addition, it can be argued that any increase in inlet valve size must be matched by an equivalent increase in exhaust valve diameter if full advantage of the improved airflow is to be taken.

For fast road use, the stock head will benefit from some judicious porting and machine work. The inlet ports themselves can be opened out by careful use of a die-grinder, although care should be taken not to remove the bump in the port which is directly below the valve spring pocket, otherwise the head will be weakened in this vital area. More radical port work will necessitate the head being welded in the area immediately above the inlet port, the extra metal allowing the port to be straightened and enlarged. This is a task best left to the experienced cylinder head specialist, although basic, non-welded, porting can be carried out at home with success using a grinding tool in an electric drill.

The exhaust ports will benefit from having the sharp radius removed from just under the valve seat, although care should be taken not to remove so much material that the seat is undercut. If this happens, there is the danger that the seat will move, especially if the valves are allowed to 'float' (through over-revving the engine) or heavy-duty valve springs are used. The overall diameter of the exhaust port need not be increased too dramatically – it is better to concentrate on removing any obvious restrictions than to go crazy with the grinding tool – and it should certainly not be opened out to the extent that the header gaskets will have a problem sealing efficiently.

Equipping the factory heads with large valves and having a professional welding and porting job carried out can result in a hefty bill from the cylinder head specialist and, in many ways, it makes more sense to start with aftermarket '042' or '044' cylinder head castings. These will be supplied with larger valves and ports straight from the shelf and will be available machined to accept 90.5/92mm or 94mm cylinders. However, they will still need to be treated to some finishing before they can be considered ready for use. The 044 castings make an excellent starting point for an efficient pair of heads for fast road use as they feature factory-style cooling fins (thus cooling is not unduly affected) and $^3/_4$in long-reach spark plugs, which help to resist cracking

This head by Adam Wik shows what can easily be done to improve a stock dual-port head for fast road use. Note how the inlet ports have been enlarged but that the vital valve spring pocket (the bump in the port next to valve guide) has not been removed.

Head has been opened out for 90.5mm cylinders and pistons and been modified to accept 42mm x 37mm valves. Combustion chamber has been reshaped to allow valves to be unshrouded for improved gas flow.

between the plug boss and the valve seats, due to the greater amount of material cast into this area.

The stock Volkswagen engine came from the factory with a very modest compression ratio – something in the region of 6.0:1 depending on the model. While this may allow you to use the very cheapest, poor quality fuel, it is not exactly conducive to making horsepower. Raising the compression is accomplished by 'fly-cutting' the cylinder heads – that is, removing material from the sealing surface around the edge of the combustion chamber, thereby reducing its volume.

On a fast road engine which sees regular use it

would be wise not to exceed a compression ratio (CR) of around 8.5:1 as the quality of fuel on offer today is not very high. Note that when aftermarket heads are used, or any new VW head, it is generally considered acceptable to use unleaded fuel, the material used for the valve seats being suitably hard. Purists may wince at the idea but in some countries, such as the USA, there is little option as leaded fuel is all but unobtainable in many areas. Raising the compression ratio is a sure way to increase horsepower as it helps to make the combustion process more efficient. However, there is a downside to running a high CR in that the cylinder head

Exhaust port has also been opened up and carefully radiused to remove the obstructive sharp bend under the valve seat. Make sure that when you install the header system, the gaskets you use have also been opened out to match the port shape.

Pauter Machine markets its 'A' head for use on fast road VWs – it is a non-welded, big-valve head with a full port and polish job. It is perfect for the person who is working to a budget and cannot afford (or does not need) a costly welded race-type head.

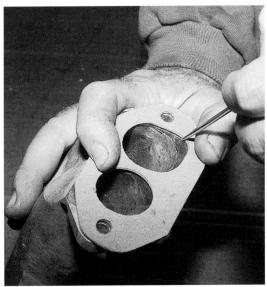

Whatever head you choose to use, you should ensure that the inlet manifold matches the shape of the inlet port. Use a gasket, along with Dychem and a scriber, to transfer the shape of the port to the manifold, then open it out with a die-grinder.

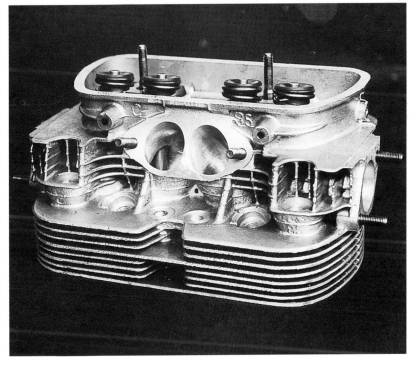

temperature will rise considerably, and detonation may result if fuel of too low an octane rating is used. Detonation is a sure-fire way to destroy an engine in no time at all – if you hear your engine starting to 'ping' under load, you are suffering detonation and need to back off that throttle to reduce the load on the engine.

Camshaft choice will be influenced by a number of factors, not the least of which is the use for which the vehicle is intended. Choosing the right camshaft for a fast road car is a fine balancing act between extracting the most from your engine combination and ensuring the end result remains

Whenever you install a new high-lift camshaft, it is vital you check there is adequate clearance between the cam lobe and the lifter when it is pushed back into its bore. There should be a minimum of 0.060in (1.5mm) clearance.

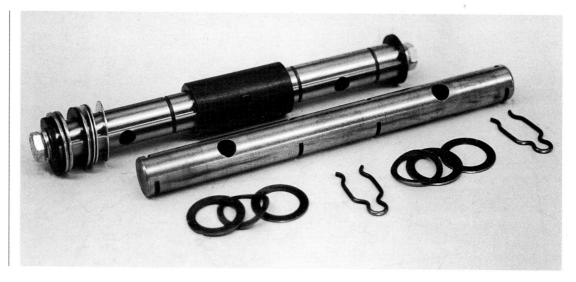

The major weakness of the stock rocker assembly is the hair-pin clip used to retain the rockers on their shaft. Buy a pair of aftermarket bolt-up rocker shafts and install your factory rocker arms – no more broken clips and loose rockers.

There are three types of tappet screw you are likely to encounter when using stock-type rocker arms. On the right is the factory plain tappet, in the center is the swivel foot (Porsche-style) and on the left is the ball-type (Ford Courier).

driveable. Fitting a cam such as an Engle FK-89 into a dual-carb 1835cc road engine may result in a combination which sounds like it is going to produce a lot of horsepower but, in reality, it will probably be a bear to drive and far from fuel-efficient. High-lift, long-duration camshafts tend, on the whole, to push the power band further up the rpm range, making an engine less pleasant to use on an everyday basis. In traffic, at low rpm, the engine may be very hesitant and you will certainly notice a significant increase in your fuel bill. It has often been said that the camshaft is the last thing you should change in an engine, and there is merit to that statement. However, if you are running a large capacity engine with big-valve heads and dual carburettors, the only way to extract the most power is to increase the cam duration and lift.

There are certain camshafts which have become almost legendary in the VW scene. Read the engine specification of many cars featured in Volkswagen magazines such as *Hot VWs* or *VolksWorld* and the titles 'Engle 110', 'Engle 120' or '125' regularly spring from the pages. This is not without reason, for these camshafts have proved themselves to be an ideal choice, time and again, in fast road engines where a balance of high horsepower and everyday driveability is expected. The Engle 110, with its duration of 284° and cam lift of 0.392", has proved to be a very popular choice for engines of 1700cc and above which run dual carburettors up to about 40mm in size. For a slightly larger engine, with a

well-prepared pair of big-valve cylinder heads, either an Engle 120 (294° duration with 0.397" lift at the cam) or a 125 (301° duration with 0.418" lift) would be a good choice – as would, of course, the equivalent camshafts from other cam suppliers.

As with any aftermarket camshaft, you will need to install new lifters (cam followers) at the same time. Most suppliers offer lifters which match their camshafts in terms of materials compatibility. With a relatively mild cam, there is no need to use anything other than a stock-type lifter, but in a more potent engine which is expected to see regular high rpm a lightweight lifter, such as that offered by Scat or Bugpack, would be a good choice.

The more radical the camshaft profile and the higher the rpm potential of the engine, the greater the need for stronger than stock valve springs if valve float is to be avoided. 'Valve float' is where the valves are held off their seats as a result of the lifters not tracking the cam lobe correctly, allowing the valves to slam shut rather than being allowed to return in a controlled manner. Nothing destroys the valve seats – or the whole valve train – quicker than valve float. It can be caused by a combination of faults, not only weak valve springs but also incorrect valve train geometry, or high-lift rocker arms being used with an incompatible camshaft.

Virtually all aftermarket performance camshafts will require the use of dual valve springs, with only the mildest of profiles allowing the owner to get away with a heavy-duty single spring. Dual valve springs are available from a number of sources, but the valve guide bosses on the stock cylinder head will need to be machined for the springs to fit. Most aftermarket heads will come ready assembled with dual springs, although it would be wise to disassemble the heads before installation to check that all is well and to carry out a good three-angle valve job (this is where the valve seats are cut with a 15° angle at the top edge, to promote better flow past the valve, along with a 60° angle to help smooth the seat into the port. Finally, a 30° angle is cut to reduce the width of the valve seat to the necessary minimum). Take nothing for granted! Often the springs supplied on some of the South American heads are not of very high quality, so it may be wise to install an alternative set from a manufacturer such as Berg or Scat. When fitting any aftermarket spring, check with the manufacturer what the correct installed height should be – this is the length of the spring once it is fitted to the cylinder head and held in place with the retainer. Too short an installed height will result in coil bind problems at full lift, while too great a height will effectively reduce the valve spring pressure. Adjustments to the installed height can be made using shims which fit under the springs.

Using a high-lift camshaft will result in a heavy side-load being exerted on the rocker arms. This can cause the weak stock 'hairpin' springs, which hold the rocker assemblies together, to break or at least come loose. When this happens, the rocker arms are free to move from side to side on the shaft, frequently allowing the pushrod to jump out of engagement, with potentially dire consequences.

To prevent this happening, if you are retaining your rocker arms, you should replace the original rocker shafts with a pair of 'bolt-up' shafts. These dispense with the stock hairpin springs and, instead, rely on a pair of bolts screwed into the ends of each shaft and a set of solid washers to hold the assembly together. At a stroke, this conversion virtually cures any problems you might have with the stock rocker arms. All aftermarket high-ratio rocker assemblies currently on the market come ready equipped with bolt-together shafts.

In addition to this fix, you should replace the stock tappet screws with a set of swivel-foot tappets

Ball-type tappet screw is strong but you must take care that there is adequate clearance between it and the rocker arm to allow correct valve setting. It may be necessary to grind the stock rocker arm slightly to gain sufficient clearance.

which prevent the tip of the valve becoming worn. If, however, you are replacing the stock rockers with a set of aftermarket assemblies, then there will be no need to do this as, in most instances, the valve lash adjustment will be made at the push-rod end of the rocker arm, a hardened pad on the rocker arm acting directly on the valve tip. To further prevent premature wear on the valve, you should also fit hardened steel 'lash caps', which not only protect the end of the valve stem but are also invaluable tools in helping to set correct valve train geometry. This is especially important where aftermarket stainless steel valves – which do not have hardened tips – are used, as is the case with the majority of replacement performance cylinder heads.

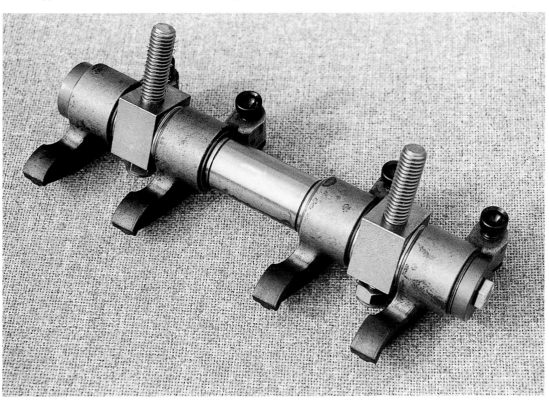

One of the best aftermarket ratio rocker assemblies is that made by Autocraft. Note how the valve adjustment is carried out at the pushrod end of the arms rather than at the valve. Other quality products are available from Berg and Pauter Machine.

Stronger valve springs will require the use of chrome-moly pushrods in place of the original aluminium ones, which are prone to bending when placed under extreme load. Whenever there have been changes to the cylinder head (eg, flycutting to increase the CR), or a change of camshaft and rocker assemblies, you will need to cut the new pushrods to length. To establish what this length should be requires the use of an adjustable dummy pushrod. Install the valves with lightweight springs – the inner spring from a dual set-up is ideal – and assemble the heads onto the completed bottom end of the engine, but leave the pushrod tubes out for the moment. Insert the adjustable pushrod (set at its shortest position) through the head and into one of the lifters and then bolt the rocker assemblies in place. Adjust the pushrod until the valve lash is just taken up and then back off to achieve 0.006in clearance.

Turn the engine over using a socket attached to the crankshaft pulley bolt (or use one of the aftermarket bolts which allows a 3/8in-drive ratchet to be attached directly) until you reach maximum valve lift. You will need to use a dial gauge to measure this accurately. Now back off until you reach the half-lift point and then check to see if the pushrod is directly in line with the adjusting screw on the rocker arm. If it isn't, then alter the length of the adjustable pushrod until it is. This will give you the required length of the new pushrods. You may need to insert shims between the rocker assemblies and the cylinder head to achieve optimum valve

train geometry – these are available in a variety of thicknesses from several suppliers. Do not underestimate the importance of establishing the correct rocker arm angles, as nothing will wear out the rockers/valves/springs etc quicker than poorly set valve train geometry. Get it badly wrong and you could end up writing off the camshaft, especially if the valve springs are allowed to reach coil bind at maximum lift.

Any fast road engine is going to be something of a compromise, being expected to deliver reliable horsepower, day in, day out. One of the most common mistakes, other than choosing too radical a camshaft, is to overestimate your carburettor requirements. Magical names like '48IDA' and 'Berg 52s' sound very attractive but, in reality, such carbs are way over the top for regular road use – unless you happen to enjoy making regular trips to the gas station. Designed more for race, or occasional all-out road use, 48IDAs and their derivatives are not the ideal choice for a street car which sees regular use, despite their legendary status among followers of the California Look faith. The main problem is that they were never really designed to be used at much other than idle or wide-open throttle on a high-performance engine.

Far better choices are either the carburettors produced by Dell'Orto (which carry the suffix 'DRLA') or Weber (suffixed 'IDF'). There have been supply problems with both these carburettor types but, in general, you shouldn't have too much problem tracking a set down. On engines up to

2 litres, we would suggest you use nothing larger than 40DRLAs or 40IDFs, although 45DRLAs and 44IDFs will work perfectly well if the engine is in a higher state of tune and gas mileage is not a prime concern. Engines over 2 litres can happily use the larger versions – if you are running a larger capacity engine and all-out performance is more your concern, then Dell'Orto also offer a 48DRLA. As far as jetting is concerned, it is not possible to make any meaningful suggestions except to have your car set up on a rolling road, or the engine run on a dyno, to establish the optimum for your engine combination. To establish a baseline setting, in order to at least get the engine running in the first place, you can follow the equation printed at the end of this chapter to find out what jet and choke sizes you should use.

If your finances don't allow you to choose a pair of Dell'Orto or Weber carburettors, then it is perfectly acceptable on an engine of under 2 litres to use a Kadron dual carb kit, produced in South America, which uses 40mm single-choke Solexes. Although you will never experience the horsepower benefits of the larger, dual-choke, carburettors, the Kadrons have proved themselves to be an excellent choice for all-round performance and driveability. Straight from the box, they work pretty well, although it is well worth the extra time and effort having the engine set up correctly on a dyno or rolling road.

When dual carburettors are fitted to any large capacity engine, the fuel demands rise dramatically, making the stock fuel pump and fuel lines marginal at best. We would recommend that you change the stock mechanical pump for an electric type, either a solid-state Facet unit or one of the interrupter-type units (also from Facet) or maybe even a Holley 'Red' pump with matching regulator. In fact, fitting a fuel-pressure regulator is a good idea whenever any electric pump is used, as both Weber and Dell'Orto carburettors are prone to flooding if the pump pressure is too high. Neither likes to see more than 3-3.5psi pressure at idle. The stock fuel line is just about adequate for most fast road engines, although if there is doubt about its condition, it would be wise to install a larger-diameter line – 1/4in or above. Make sure your stock fuel tank vent is not blocked or, preferably, replace it with a vent pipe which is at least as large in diameter as the fuel line if fuel starvation is to be avoided at high rpm.

Any engine which has seen a capacity increase, been equipped with dual carburettors and reworked cylinder heads and had an aftermarket camshaft fitted, will not produce its optimum power unless attention is paid to the exhaust system. The stock muffler is fine for very mild engines which have not been increased in size, but as soon as you ask the engine to 'breathe' more air and burn more fuel, then it will become a power-sapping restriction. In an ideal world, you should remove the stock heater

Now, while this may look pretty, all that chrome plating won't help the engine to stay cool. Avoid using chrome tinware on your engine – the factory chose a black finish for a good reason: it helps to dissipate heat far more efficiently.

Any performance engine needs to breathe, and that means having a free-flowing exhaust system. The current vogue is to use a 'turbo' muffler. Here, we are offering up a muffler and pipework to check for clearance under the rear apron.

As the turbo mufflers are quite heavy, it is vital you attach a support strap to take the strain off the rest of the system. This can be bolted to the bumper mounting under the rear wing. Flexible strap allows for engine movement.

Large diameter of exhaust pipe means that you may need to use 8mm-thread nuts which have been made for use with an 11mm spanner (normally 13mm). These special nuts are available from several sources, including Bugpack.

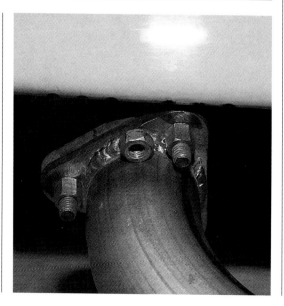

boxes at the same time as you replace the main exhaust system as the inside diameter of the exhaust pipes running through them is too small – like the stock muffler itself, the heater boxes were never intended to flow any more gases than those produced by a stock engine. In reality, if you wish to retain a heating system in your VW, you have little option but to use them, although you will never achieve the best results from your engine, and prolonged use may cause the exhaust valves to burn due to the restriction in the exhaust system. If heating is not a problem, then replace the boxes with a pair of J-pipes, or fit a competition-style header system which dispenses with the heating system. Alternatively, it is possible to use the old 'non-fresh air' style of heater boxes, modified to accept large-diameter header pipes. The heater boxes fitted to 34bhp (US 40hp) Beetles built prior to December 1962 may be modified in this manner.

As far as the design and size (ie, diameter) of the header pipes are concerned, until recently the most popular choices were either single or dual 'quiet' muffler systems mounted on a 1.5in (up to 2 litres) or 1.625in system (2 litres and above). Several such systems are on offer from all the major suppliers, but be aware that not all are true 'merged' systems, the design of which helps to scavenge the exhaust gases more efficiently. Non-merged systems are usually referred to simply as extractor exhausts and, while certainly less restrictive than a stock muffler set-up, they should not be considered the ultimate. Avoid low-cost glass-pack muffler systems as they do little other than make a lot of noise.

To keep your engine's flame burning bright, you will need a good ignition system. In most cases, on engines which are expected to produce around 100-

Turbo mufflers may not be the prettiest of components but tests show that they are far less restrictive than the conventional quiet-pack or glasspack mufflers. A coat of heat-resistant paint will help to prevent the system from rusting.

120bhp, a Bosch 009 distributor and matching high-energy Bosch Blue coil are all that is needed, along with a good set of plug leads. The 009 has become the mainstay of the industry, taking over from the better quality 010 unit, which is now no longer in production. Both the 009 and the 010 are well-suited to the hot VW engine, retaining the factory spark retard to number 3 cylinder, and have an advance curve which has proved almost universally ideal for most applications. There are kits available which convert your 009 to pointless electronic ignition and these are certainly worth considering, especially when your car sees frequent use or is regularly revved to over 6,000rpm, where points bounce can become a problem. As for plug leads, there are several options open to you but, in general, a new set of so-called silicone leads is fine.

Spark plug choice is a matter of great debate among engine builders, with each favouring certain brands and heat ranges. From the factory, VWs came with Bosch spark plugs with a type number 145T1 (now classified as W6AC). When an engine is modified, the combustion temperatures generally rise, necessitating the use of a 'colder' plug if pre-ignition is to be avoided (ie, the fuel being ignited too soon due to the spark plug remaining hot after the previous combustion cycle). The next colder plug in Bosch's range is the 175T1 (or W7AC), followed by the 225T1 (or W6AC). Note these are for use with cylinder heads which accept the stock-type 14mm, $1/2$ in reach plugs – heads which require long-reach plugs (such as the '044' heads) will require a different type of plug. Consult your supplier to find the equivalent grade.

So, to recap on our fast road engine: use a late-model, dual-relief valve crankcase which has been drilled and tapped for an external oil system. The case will need to be clearanced to accept a stroker crank and bored for larger cylinders. For reliable road use, a 78mm crank is ideal, used in conjunction with 90.5mm cylinders and pistons. Stock, or Rimco 'Super-Rods' or similar can be used to good effect. Use either reworked factory dual-port heads with larger valves (40mm x 35.5mm for up to 2-litres) or good quality aftermarket castings, such as the '044' type, set at no more than 9.0:1 compression. Dual Dell'Orto 40DRLA or Weber 40IDF carburettors, with a quality Berg or Tayco linkage, and an electric fuel pump with regulator should be installed. Avoid using a cheap extractor exhaust with glasspack muffler, and instead choose a quality merged system with single or dual quiet mufflers. Install a Bosch 009 distributor, preferably with pointless electronic ignition. As for the camshaft and valve-train, err on the mild side with an Engle 120 or 125, chrome-moly pushrods and a bolt-together rocker assembly with swivel-feet tappet screws.

Such a combination, correctly assembled and with professionally reworked cylinder heads, should offer in the region of 100-110bhp, possibly more, reliably and with little drama. It will also be an ideal stepping stone to bigger and better things…

STRENGTHENING THE TRANSMISSION
How to make the most of your new-found horsepower

With something in the region of 100-120bhp at your disposal, it is not unreasonable to suspect that there will be times when you will succumb to the temptation to make full use of it, either on the street or at the track. As mentioned in the mild street

Installing a Super-Diff is a good starting point as far as beefing up your transmission is concerned. The one shown on the left is a screw-type swing-axle unit, that on the right a snap-ring style. Note both are drilled to accept either early or late ring gear.

This is an IRS Super-Diff – compare this with the photograph of the stock IRS differential unit in section one of this book; the casing of the Super-Diff is considerably stronger. However, the weakness of the splined output shaft remains.

section, the most likely problem areas are the differential and the axles, although it has to be said that you would need to be extremely unlucky to break an axle unless relentlessly pursuing that elusive ET at the drag strip.

The stock VW differential unit is more than adequately strong for its intended use but, as it has only two spider gears to carry the load, there is a tendency for them to break. This usually happens when you drop the clutch and cause one wheel to spin (not being a limited slip differential, there is no way to control the distribution of power to the wheels). This places an extremely heavy load on the spider gears, which fail, rendering the car immobile. As with all transmission failures, it is guaranteed to happen at the worst possible moment when you are miles from home…

In an effort to prevent this happening, there are so-called Beef-A-Diff kits on the market which add an extra pair of spider gears to the otherwise stock differential unit. Unfortunately, this is not the answer as these extra gears are not supported properly and fail almost as easily. The correct solution is to fit a Super-Diff, a heavy-duty differential casing which contains four spider gears, each pair properly located on a hardened shaft. In all but the most extreme situations this will solve your differential problems.

There are two styles of Super-Diffs available for the swing-axle transmission: snap-ring and screw-in. The former holds the side gears in place with a heavy-duty snap-ring, which locates in a groove machined inside the diff housing, while the latter relies on a threaded ring which screws into the diff housing. Both styles have their advocates, although the snap-ring type is generally more popular. Some companies machine the housing to make space for an extra snap-ring in an effort to prevent the side gears from being forced away from the spider gears under load. For fast road use, a regular snap-ring Super-Diff should be more than adequate.

If you are running an IRS transmission, in a Super Beetle, for example, it is possible to buy a heavy-duty differential housing with an extra pair of spider gears ready to accept the two stock gears and the combined side gears and output shafts. The IRS set-up offers the advantage of superior handling, as

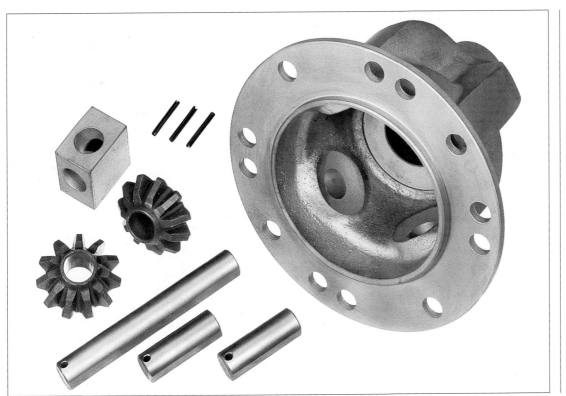

the rear wheels do not suffer the same radical camber changes as the swing-axle design. However, there are four potential points of weakness to be considered in the IRS design: the CV joints. In stock form these are fine but they are prone to failure when allowed to run dry (check the condition of the rubber boots on a regular basis) or when subjected to extreme abuse. The axles themselves rarely fail but the same cannot be said of the output shafts from the gearbox, which are an integral part of the side gears. Side-step the clutch once too often on a dry road and eventually the output shaft will fail at the base of the splined section where the CV-joint flange locates.

Virtually all Super-Diffs require a slight modification before they are ready for the road – the oiling hole in the casing will more often than not need to be enlarged with a drill to allow more oil to lubricate the spider gears. This is a common fault with Super-Diffs but this modification appears to solve the problem of the spider gears being starved of lubricant. Installing a Super-Diff is not out of the question for the home mechanic, just so long as he or she has access to the necessary shims and measuring equipment needed to set the pre-load on the transmission sideplates. In simple terms, installation requires the removal of the right-hand sideplate, which allows the differential and crown-wheel to be removed, transferring the crown-wheel to the Super-Diff and reinstalling as a new unit. The skill lies with setting the correct amount of preload on the sideplate, which dictates how closely the teeth of the ring and pinion are held in mesh.

On a street car, the preload should be in the region of 0.004-0.006in (0.10-0.15mm), while a

race car will need a preload of 0.012in (0.3mm).

To help keep the ring and pinion together, a heavy-duty sideplate can be fitted. You only need to install one such plate and make sure you fit it to the right side of the gearbox (the crown-wheel side). The idea behind this is that the stock cast sideplate is not strong enough, allowing the ring (crown-wheel) and pinion to move out of mesh slightly as the sideplate flexes under load. This will eventually lead to the ring and pinion failing. Heavy-duty

The Beef-A-Diff unit is not worth considering as it does little to strengthen the transmission. All it does is to add a second pair of spider gears to the stock diff housing but the extra gears are not adequately supported.

One of the weak links on the Volkswagen transmission is the sideplate, which is designed to prevent the crown wheel from coming out of mesh with the pinion. The stock swing-axle component, seen here on the right, is far weaker than the aftermarket type on the left.

sideplates are available off the shelf to fit both swing-axle and IRS transmissions from a variety of suppliers.

Another modification that is worth carrying out is to fit what Gene Berg Enterprises refer to as their 'Poor Man's Posi' – actually a selection of shims which are installed between the side gears of the differential unit and the snap-ring retainers. This pre-loads the spider gears and, to some degree, tricks the stock differential into working like a limited slip differential. It also ensures that the spider gears

remain in mesh with one another while under severe load. An inexpensive trick, it can be duplicated by the use of a selection of carefully trimmed crankshaft end-float shims.

The matter of whether to change the gear ratios on a street car all depends on what kind of driving you do and what you are really expecting from your car. If all you ever use your fast road VW for is a quick blast around town once or twice a week, or you enjoy taking your car to the drag strip occasionally, then fitting close-ratio third and fourth

Heavy-duty sideplates are also available for the IRS transmissions. The stock sideplate is shown here on the right, alongside the aftermarket replacement. Note the more susbtantial design of the latter, notably around the outer edge.

In addition to a stronger sideplate, you can also install steel support rings to prevent the pressed steel sidecovers on a swing-axle trans from distorting. They can also be used with a stock sideplate to provide some extra strength.

An inexpensive modification is to install Berg's Poor Man's Posi – basically a set of shims which help to preload the side gears of a swing-axle transmission, preventing excessive movement of the gears and reducing the risk of the snap-ring coming loose.

gears may be just the ticket. They will allow you to make full use of the available power of your new engine by letting you keep it in the power band while shifting up through the gears. However, if you envisage using the car for lengthy freeway journeys, or you are after optimum fuel economy, then close-ratio gears are not for you (at least, not in a conventional four-speed VW transmission).

Most close-ratio conversions for the street involve fitting new third and fourth gear sets, bringing the ratios down and closer to the stock first and second. This is a relatively straightforward operation, although it does naturally involve a complete tear-down of the transmission, which may be something best left to an experienced specialist. The temptation is to fit ultra-close ratios so that the car feels like a true race car on the street, but this may not prove to be a wise move in the long run. Driving a car with a very low fourth gear for more

Aftermarket close-ratio gear on right is by Gem in the USA. Note how the teeth are deeper and cut at less of a helix (the angle of the teeth). This makes the gear stronger but also more noisy in operation.

The two types of pinion shaft used in VW transmissions: splined and key-way. Both are interchangeable but some people feel that the key-way design, which uses a large nut in place of a snap-ring, is superior.

You should weld the synchro hubs on 3rd and 4th gears, rather than relying on the factory interference fit. If left alone, the synchro hubs can spin under power, losing drive. Welds should then be ground down flush on a belt sander.

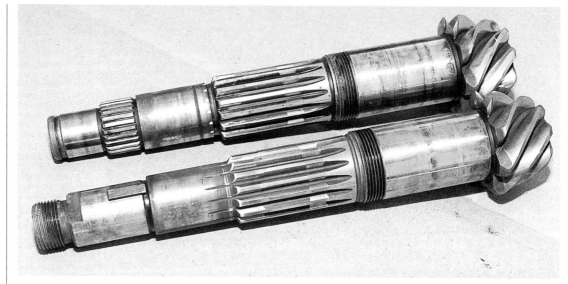

than a short distance can become tiresome very quickly: noise levels inside the car are significantly increased; fuel consumption increases dramatically, as does engine wear, and the whole car may tend to feel uncomfortable to use on a regular basis.

A popular solution is to choose a set of ratios which retain the stock first and second, have a significantly lower third gear and a fourth gear which is only slightly lower than stock. This way you gain the benefit of close ratios through the first three gears but you can then cruise in a top gear which is not far removed from the original. OK, so there is a larger gap between third and fourth than if you had chosen an ultra-low top gear but you won't really notice the difference that much. However, you will appreciate the ability to drive your street car for more than just a few miles at a time. Also, most exhibitions of speed at the stop light (and, of course, we're not talking of street racing here because that is something we cannot possibly condone…) see the action taking place through first, second and third gears. By the time you shift into top, it's all over, bar the bench-racing afterwards.

The one problem you may run into when installing new third and fourth gears is that the later mainshaft (with its stronger 3.78:1 first gear) will not accept many of the available aftermarket ratios: the pre-1972 mainshafts had keyways machined into them for a Woodruff key, which located third and fourth gears, whereas the later mainshafts were splined. Virtually all aftermarket gear ratios available today are of the earlier keyed type, meaning that the mainshaft needs to be turned down on a lathe and a keyway cut to accept the Woodruff key. Fortunately, the later mainshaft is slightly larger in diameter round the splined area, allowing it to be machined to suit the early-style gear sets.

If you plan on getting serious with your Beetle, then there are some other modifications that are worth making to the transmission while it is apart. First of all, have third and fourth gears welded to the synchromesh hubs, rather than relying on the factory interference fit. This a relatively straightforward procedure, which will prevent the gears from spinning on the synchro hubs under load. However, the welds need to be ground back flush with the face of the gear using a belt sander or a surface grinder. On the factory 'box, there is a heavy spring spacer between third and fourth gears which, while perfectly satisfactory for stock situations, can

Originally built in the 1970s, Dave Kanase's sedan perfectly captures the spirit of a fast road car: mild suspension modifications, an uprated engine and a purposeful, no-nonsense look. The car is still going strong over 20 years later.

In some cases, you may
need to clearance the inside
of the intermediate housing
of the transmission to take
into account the larger
outside diameter of some
close-ratio gear sets. The
clearancing required is
minimal.

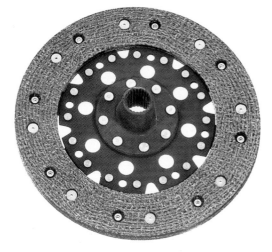

*In general, a stock-type clutch disc is more than adequate for a
fast road car, although you should use the solid (non-sprung)
type as it is stronger. Woven Pro-Grip disc is not really
necessary as factory style is perfectly adequate.*

allow the gears to move on the pinion shaft. An
aftermarket solid spacer is available for heavy-duty
use and this will cure any potential ills. The stock
Woodruff keys are too soft and, once again, heavy-
duty aftermarket chrome-moly replacements should
be used. Furthermore, you should also replace the
stock gear selector forks with aftermarket steel parts

to prevent them bending while shifting hard.

At this level of tuning, axle breakage need not
be a major concern – the stock axles are very high
quality and can stand a tremendous amount of
abuse. Of course, there will always come a point
when over-exuberance leads to a breakage, but the
limits are fairly high. To get the maximum life out of
your stock axles, you should always reinstall them in
the same way in which they were removed from the
transmission: the right-hand-side axle must be used
on the right side of the car, the left-hand-side on the
left. This is because the axles take on a 'set', actually
twisting slightly with use. Reversing their direction
of rotation will cause them to fail far sooner.

You could also spend some time polishing the
axles, especially around the spade end which locates
in the differential side gears. If an axle is going to
break, it will always fail at this point – the axle just
happens to be at its weakest here. Polishing out all
the forging marks on a belt sander or with a flap
wheel mounted in an electric drill will help to
relieve stress build-up in the axles. Time consuming,
yes, but worth it in the long run.

When it comes to mounting your transmission
in your VW, there are several options open to you.
The main objective is to limit the movement of the
engine and gearbox as far as possible. The ultimate
way is to fit solid transmission mountings but, for

Kennedy Engineering Products (KEP) manufactures this high-quality diaphragm clutch pressure plate which offers 2700lb of 'grab' pressure but without causing a heavy clutch pedal. Note flywheel has been lightened on this engine.

A simple way to help prevent excessive engine movement is to install a traction bar under the rear of the engine case. This is supported by a pair of rods which locate on brackets bolted to the inner wing.

the purpose of a regularly driven fast-road VW, the drawback is excessive noise inside the car and increased vibration, which may lead to certain parts working themselves loose. By far the simplest solution is to install a rear engine hanger, or traction bar, as it is usually called. This is nothing more than a strong, square-section steel tube which is hung from two threaded supports. The bar passes under the rear of the crankcase, adjacent to the oil pump, and prevents the engine from dropping as the car accelerates.

However, if you wish to take things a stage further, you can replace the stock mountings with a set of urethane mouldings, which deform far less than the original rubber components. These urethane mountings locate the transmission more

Bugpack, among others, manufactures a set of urethane transmission mountings which are far more rigid than the stock rubber type. However, they should be periodically checked for cracks. Noise levels inside the car will be increased.

rigidly but at the expense of slightly increased noise inside the car. They have also been known to crack and split with use, so will need to be checked regularly. In general, for a car which produces around 100-120bhp and only sees casual strip use (on radial tyres, not slicks) probably the best all-round solution is simply to install new factory mountings and a well-made traction bar. This is a tried and tested combination which offers the best of both worlds: firm transaxle location and little increase in noise.

UPRATING THE SUSPENSION
Why slow down for the corners?

It's all very well having a car with an engine which produces three times the original power output but to get the most out of it you are going to need to uprate the suspension fairly drastically. There is nothing more frustrating than exploring the limits of your Beetle's straight-line performance, only to have to slam on the brakes at the first sight of a corner. Similarly, what's the point of heading to the drag strip if your 120 new-found horses are going to try to rip the back of the car apart by inducing incurable wheel hop?

Looking at the Beetle suspension as a whole, there really cannot be too much wrong if the same basic concept was used by Porsche on its successful 356 models until the mid-1960s. If anyone was going to make a break from torsion bars front and rear while in search of superior handling, it would have been Porsche. Even if your Beetle's suspension is kept entirely as the factory intended, apart from the simple upgrade of a set of aftermarket shock-absorbers, you will be able to enjoy your car on

The process of lowering the rear of a Beetle is essentially the same whether the car has swing-axle or IRS suspension. You will need to remove the bolts holding the spring plates to the rear hub carrier (axle tubes on a swing axle car).

The bolts retaining the torsion bar cover also need to be removed, allowing you to lever the spring plate off its stop. Check the condition of the rubber bushes which support the outer end of the torsion bar and replace if necessary.

The torsion bar may be rotated in its splines at the inner end and the spring plate rotated on the outer splines to finely adjust the ride height. An alternative solution is to install adjustable spring plates which allow ride height changes at the turn of a spanner.

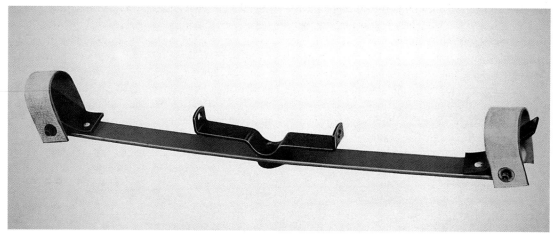

twisty roads far more than you ever imagined. But, to make the most of its hidden potential, your VW needs to have some serious attention paid to several areas of the suspension.

Starting at the rear of the car, one of the most beneficial modifications you can carry out, especially to a swing-axle Beetle, is to lower – or 'decamber' – the suspension. In standard form, the rear suspension of a swing-axle Beetle is set with slight positive camber when the vehicle is stationary, which changes to negative camber when a load is placed on the car (increased weight or when accelerating). This is fine when the car is only expected to be used as a family run-around but is hopeless if the car is pushed hard into a corner. With the slightest positive camber at the back wheels, the outside rear wheel will want to tuck under the car, causing the back end to lose grip.

To a certain degree, this can be overcome by installing stiffer shock-absorbers, which will tend to resist any movement of the suspension. But, to come as close to curing the problem as is possible, you are going to need to reset the rear suspension so that the wheels start out with a slight negative camber. That way, when the outer wheel of the car is loaded when negotiating a bend, it is less likely to want to tuck under and create excessive positive camber, preferring instead to keep the tyre more fully in contact with the road surface.

Assuming that everything is in good order, decambering the rear of a Beetle need cost you no money, just a little of your time. Begin by raising the back end of the car and removing the rear wheels, making sure that the car is properly supported on axle stands and level, side to side. You will need to undo the three large nuts and bolts which hold the axle tube (or semi-trailing arm and hub carrier on an IRS car) to the spring plate. Next, you must undo the four bolts which retain the torsion bar cover plate (located at the front end of the spring plate) and remove it, along with the rubber bush which supports the end of the torsion bar.

You must now gently lever the spring plate off its rebound stop and allow it to hang free on the end of the torsion bar. Do not remove it or the torsion bar at this point. With a sharp chisel, mark the position of the spring plate on the torsion bar. To achieve a drop of around 2.5ins, you can remove the spring plate from the torsion bar and move it round by one spline. The spring plate can now be levered, or jacked, back onto the rebound stop and the bush and torsion bar cover replaced. With the suspension reassembled and the car on level ground, you will notice that the rear wheels will now have a few degrees of negative camber. You may need to trim the bump stops (snubbers) a little to prevent the suspension from bottoming out if you carry any passengers.

Now, it may be that you don't want to lower the car so much – excessive lowering can result in the rear hub bearings running dry of oil as they are supplied with gearbox lubricant which simply runs down the axle tubes to the bearings. Excessive

negative camber will mean that the oil would have to flow uphill to reach the bearings, something that the laws of gravity won't allow, even on a Beetle!

To allow you to fine tune the rear ride height, as mentioned in the introductory chapter, Volkswagen made the torsion bars with different numbers of splines on the inner and outer ends (40 and 44 respectively). Carefully removing the torsion bar and turning it three splines at the inner end and then turning the spring plate in the opposite direction by a further three splines will result in a change in angle of the spring plate of 2.5°. This is sufficient to give slight negative camber at the rear wheels with little or no loss of ride quality. Increase this to four-splines 'each way' and the angle becomes slightly over 3.25°, resulting in a reduction in ride height of around 1.5ins. In most instances, this is perfect for improved handling, with none of the drawbacks associated with more radical lowering. Incidentally, lowering the rear suspension won't necessitate fitting shorter shock absorbers as there is more than enough available travel.

To combat the dreaded swing-axle 'tuck under', the American company EMPI developed what it referred to as a 'camber compensator' in the early 1960s. This device was designed to limit the amount by which the rear wheels could adopt positive camber while negotiating a bend. Consisting of little more than an interconnecting spring between the two rear axle shafts, located in the center by a bracket bolted to the transmission, the camber compensator worked extremely well and proved to be a popular product throughout the 1960s. Today, a similar device is offered by a number of suppliers, the design having been updated slightly by the addition of urethane bushes. It is, without doubt, a very worthwhile addition to any swing-axle Beetle.

Another very simple device, which was originally developed for the drag racer to prevent the rear suspension from unloading too far and allowing the wheels to develop positive camber, is the so-called 'flop-stop'. This is little more than a U-shaped piece of metal which is clamped to the spring plate adjacent to the rebound stop. All it does is reduce the available downward movement of the rear suspension, thereby preventing the onset of positive camber. Like the camber compensator, it is simple but effective and without any undesirable side-effects.

The owner of an IRS Beetle can make a considerable improvement to the way his car handles by installing a rear sway (anti-roll) bar. This is available from Sway-A-Way and comes complete with all parts to allow installation on any IRS Beetle, including semi-automatic 'stickshift' models. Fitting is straightforward and requires only the use of basic hand tools. The result is a car which corners with far less body roll than a stocker, but this aftermarket sway bar must be used with an uprated front bar.

There are further ways to improve the rear suspension of the Beetle, notably by replacing the rubber bushes in both the swing-axle and the IRS systems. On both models, there are rubber bushes on either side of the spring plate, by the torsion bar, and these can be swapped for the harder urethane

A swing-axle car can be converted to IRS rear suspension by welding on the necessary brackets to accept the semi-trailing arms. Bolt-on conversion kits are also available, but cannot be recommended. (Note: chassis has been turned upside down for ease of photography.)

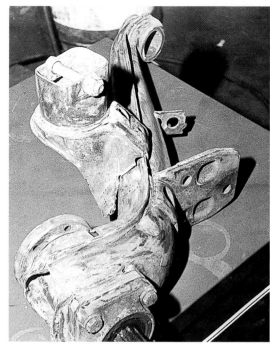

Urethane bushes are available to replace the stock rubber torsion bar bushes which are usually worn out after many years of hard work. The bushes, from Bugpack or Sway-A-Way, help prevent unwanted movement of the spring plate.

If you are lowering the front of your king- and link-pin Beetle by more than a couple of inches, you will need to remove the bump stops. Ideally they should be rewelded in a higher position, although many people dispense with them altogether.

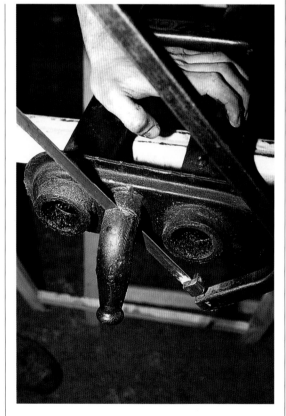

Radically lowering the rear of an IRS Beetle will still result in negative camber on the back wheels. To cure this, you can swap the semi-trailing arms from side to side but you must cut off the shock-absorber mounts and reweld them in the correct position.

type, available from Sway-A-Way and Bugpack, the latter marketing its products under the Prothane banner. Note that the inner and outer bushes are different and cannot be interchanged. Any movement of the spring plate fore and aft will have an adverse effect on the way in which a car handles, and installing urethane bushes will make the rear end of the car feel more solid as they will help to preserve suspension geometry more accurately. The rear of an IRS Beetle can be improved still further by replacing the bush at the inner end of the semi-trailing arm with a new urethane moulding. Note,

however, that urethane bushes are notorious for squeaking when dry. To help prevent this, spray a little silicone lubricant on the bushes when you install them.

At the front end of the Beetle, the act of lowering the suspension is slightly more time-consuming and costly, as you will need to buy certain parts regardless of whether you are planning any other changes, such as the installation of urethane bushes. Both the early king- and link-pin and the later ball-joint suspension systems are lowered in exactly the same way, with only the Super Beetle's MacPherson strut system requiring a totally different approach. To lower the front end of a torsion bar Beetle, you need either to install one or other of the proprietary torsion bar adjusters (commonly referred to as Sway-A-Ways after the company which introduced them) or a pair of dropped spindles.

Lowering the suspension of a car usually means that there will be a loss of ride quality, this being the result of a reduction in suspension travel and a change in steering geometry. All too often, a radically lowered Beetle will prove to be very uncomfortable to drive, with a very harsh ride and excessive bump steer. However, this need not be the case. When a car is lowered by conventional methods, travel is reduced, with the suspension components coming into contact with the bump stops sooner, giving the bone-shaking ride which characterizes many custom Beetles. By installing dropped spindles, a car may be lowered without any

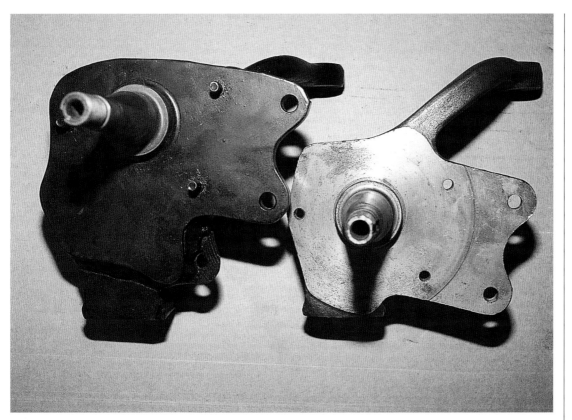

Whenever you lower the suspension by conventional methods, there will be some loss of ride quality due to the reduction in available wheel travel. There is a way round this: install a pair of dropped spindles. Those shown are for ball-joint VWs with disc brakes.

Dropped spindles are also available for link-pin models. Note how the spindle is mounted 2-3ins higher in relation to the steering arm. The main disadvantage of dropped spindles is that they offer no form of suspension ride-height adjustment.

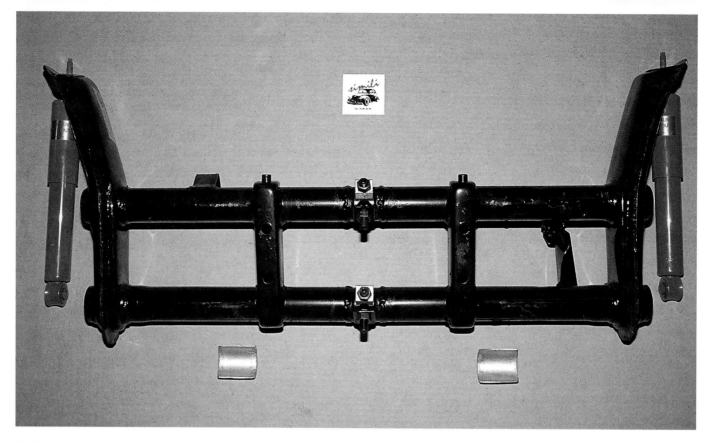

Shown here is a ball-joint front beam with Sway-A-Ways installed. When lowering the suspension, you need to install shorter shock absorbers such as the KYB units shown. This is necessary to prevent the shock absorbers bottoming out.

When lowering a ball-joint car, one of the dangers is that the ball-joints will run out of travel, resulting in premature wear and possible failure. To combat this, you should install long-travel ball-joints, available from most specialists.

effect whatsoever on ride quality. Dropped spindles are front suspension forgings where the stub axle is relocated 2.5ins higher, having the effect of raising the wheel in relation to the suspension (thereby lowering the car). However, because there has been no other change to the suspension geometry, the car rides and steers like a stocker.

At first sight, fitting dropped spindles appears to be the ideal way in which to lower your Beetle but,

as with most things, there is a down side. With other forms of lowering, there is scope for some adjustment of the ride height – with dropped spindles there is none. Another disadvantage is that many dropped spindle conversions are made by machining off part of the stub axle assembly and welding a new stub axle in place. The way in which this is carried out results in an increase in wheel track, pushing the tyres out and closer to the fenders. This can be a problem if wider wheels and tyres have been installed.

The alternatives to dropped spindles are the weld-in adjusters. In the old days, the favoured product was the Select-A-Drop, a rather crude device which twisted the upper set of torsion leaves round so that the front of the car was pulled down. Select-A-Drops were originally designed for use with lightweight glassfibre buggies in which ride quality was not a primary concern. When installed in a sedan, a Select-A-Drop would result in a very stiff ride.

Prior even to the Select-A-Drop, the most popular method of dropping the front suspension of a Beetle was to remove some of the torsion leaves from the axle beam. This was achieved by welding the leaves together at each end, and either side of the central location, and then cutting out some of the small leaves, and occasionally one or two of the

large ones. The result was a dumped front end but, once again, at the expense of a terrible ride. Alternatively, and slightly more scientifically, some people tried cutting the center section from each front torsion beam, before turning and rewelding it. This allowed the car to be lowered, but it was very hit or miss, and again made no provision for adjustment.

However, the basic concept of rotating the center mounting point of the torsion leaves was sound and this idea eventually developed into the torsion bar adjusters which are so popular today. These adjusters may be installed once the axle beam has been removed from the car and disassembled. Using the adjuster as a guide, mark the section of the torsion beams and cut them out with a hacksaw or tubing cutter. The adjusters are welded in place (check the illustrations for details of the correct position and angle) and the whole assembly reinstalled in the car. Adjustment of the ride height can now be carried out by simply unlocking and turning a pair of socket-head bolts. Wind them out and the car will be lowered, screw them in and the car is raised, as simple as that. When lowering the car more than an inch or two, you will need to install shorter shock absorbers to prevent them from bottoming out – these are available from several sources and in styles to suit either link-pin or ball-joint front ends. When excessively lowering a link-pin Beetle, you may need to relocate, or even remove, the stock bump stop. The drawback with this is that there is an increased risk of damage to the shock absorbers and tie rod ends.

The limiting factor, other than the shock absorbers, on a ball-joint Beetle is the available travel in the ball-joints themselves. It is all too easy to lower a post-'65 Beetle to the point where the stock ball-joints run out movement and bind solid, leading almost inevitably to their eventual failure. To combat this, it is possible to purchase long-travel ball-joints from most VW specialists which allow far greater suspension travel without binding. These should be installed as a matter of course on any lowered ball-joint Beetle.

Torsion bar adjusters – 'Sway-A-Ways', if you will – are by far the most popular method used to drop the front end of a Beetle and probably the most versatile. In many ways, the perfect way to lower your Beetle is to install a pair of Sway-A-Ways and a pair of dropped spindles. That way you get the best of both worlds: the superior ride of a car with near-stock suspension travel and the ability to fine-tune the ride height. Sure, the cost is considerably higher than choosing one method or the other, but who said perfection was cheap?

While the axle beam is apart, you should consider replacing the stock needle bearings at each end of the torsion tubes with some urethane mouldings. These are self-lubricating and long-lasting, offering better support to the trailing arms than 30- or 40-year old worn bearings. You could also install urethane bump stops, although on a regular road car these are not a major priority.

When lowering a torsion bar Beetle more than an inch or so, it will be necessary to add a pair of shims behind the lower torsion tube to restore the

Sway-A-Way torsion bar adjusters for the front suspension have become the industry standard. There are two types available: the one on the right is to fit king- and link-pin Beetles, that on the left is for ball-joint models.

The Sway-A-Ways can be installed in one or both torsion beams of the front axle and allow the ride height to be adjusted very easily. The axle beam needs to be removed from the car and disassembled before installation.

With the torsion leaves removed, the center is removed from the axle beam with a hacksaw, making sure that the cuts are accurate and exactly to the width of the Sway-A-Way. Clean any grease and old paint from around cuts.

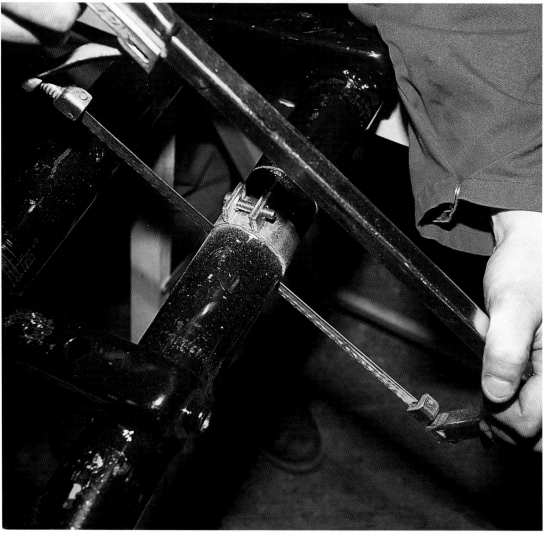

The adjusters are welded in place using a MIG-welder. For extra strength and better weld penetration, you should chamfer the edges of the cut prior to welding. Tack weld in place first and then final weld only when you're sure everything is correctly aligned.

To make certain each adjuster is welded in place at the same angle, you can make a simple template out of stiff cardboard. Note that the adjusting screws of the Sway-A-Ways should face downwards.

There are alternatives to the use of Sway-A-Ways, including Berg's Avis adjuster which doesn't require the beam to be cut. A similar design is used on the South American Puma axle beams, which come ready fitted with adjusters.

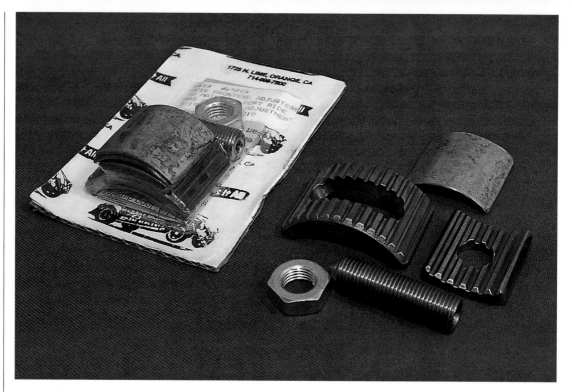

If you are only lowering the front end of your car, the resultant nose-down rake will remove the caster angle from the front suspension, making the car very 'nervous' in a straight line. It is vital that steps are taken to restore the caster angle.

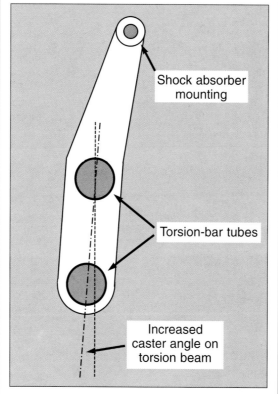

Shock absorber mounting

Torsion-bar tubes

Increased caster angle on torsion beam

caster angle. This is the angle of the line drawn through the king-pin, on an early Beetle, or between the upper and lower ball-joints on a later model, compared with vertical. Stock Beetles have just over 2° of caster on the axle beam (equating to a little over 4° of king-pin inclination), which is necessary to give the car greater stability in a straight line. As soon as you lower the front end of a car, this angle diminishes and the self-centering effect is reduced, causing the car to become rather nervous on a straight piece of road. Drag racers have

known all about this for years and have spaced out the lower torsion tube to restore the caster angle, or even increase it. On all but the most radically lowered cars, one pair of spacers is adequate, although two may be necessary if your car has a distinct nose-down stance. Note, however, that the greater the caster angle, the heavier the steering will become.

Lowering a MacPherson strut Beetle requires an altogether different approach. Basically, there are two options available: simply installing shorter springs or replacing the entire strut with an adjustable aftermarket alternative. The former will allow you to lower the car by a couple of inches without too much loss of ride quality, but for the best results you should fit new aftermarket struts. These are available with an adjustable lower spring cup which allows you to move the spring up and down the strut leg to alter the ride height. These struts are generally shorter than stock and require a new shorter insert (effectively, the shock-absorber) to be installed. Typically, this will be one from a VW Golf, which makes it both inexpensive and readily available. Installing adjustable front struts is, without doubt, one of the best modifications you can make to your Super Beetle.

Another problem you will almost certainly run into when driving a lowered Beetle is the phenomenon known as 'bump-steer'. On a stock Beetle, the tie rods are virtually parallel to the ground (when viewed from the front of the car) and are designed to move up and down in an arc with suspension movement. As the wheels rise or drop to the limits of their travel, the effective distance between the steering box and the stub axle assemblies is reduced. Because the tie rods are

Just visible between the lower axle beam and the frame head of the chassis is a pair of caster shims, installed on this Beetle in an effort to make it more stable in a straight line. Normally, only one set of shims is necessary but two are often used on race cars.

Urethane has definitely become the material of choice, with virtually every suspension bush being available in this self-lubricating, hard-wearing material. These are heavy-duty trailing arm bushes which replace the factory bearings in the front axle.

located behind the center line of the wheels, the result is that the wheels are made to adopt a certain degree of toe-out. The more the wheels are deflected from their normal position, the greater the effect will be.

On a Beetle which has been lowered, the tie rods will adopt an upwards inclination towards the wheels, even when at rest – now any slight change in position of the wheel will have a significant effect on the steering geometry, causing the car to become quite unstable over an undulating surface. This is bump-steer, and it can be felt through the steering wheel by the driver: the wheel kicks back and forth in the driver's hands.

Lowering a Super Beetle, with its MacPherson strut front end, needs an altogether different approach to that used on a Beetle with torsion bar front suspension. This slammed 1303 looks particularly fine with its polished Porsche Fuchs alloy wheels.

The simplest way to drop the front of a MacPherson strut Beetle is to cut the coil springs or simply install shorter aftermarket ones. This isn't the best way to go as you will soon run out of suspension travel; it is better to use shorter struts.

On a stock Beetle, the tie rod ends are located in the steering arms from the top. By inserting them from below, the angle of the tie rods is greatly reduced. To do this, you should install a bump-steer kit, which consists of a pair of bushes, the insides of which have been machined with a taper to match that of the tie-rod ends. Drill or ream out the old taper from the steering arm and press the new bushes in from below. You can now reinstall the tie-rod ends from underneath. This simple conversion will solve virtually all instances of bump-steer, greatly improving the straight-line stability of your lowered VW.

The one other major improvement that can be made on any Beetle, torsion bar or MacPherson strut, is to install an uprated sway (anti-roll) bar. These are available in a number of diameters, the thicker the bar, the stiffer it becomes. A stronger anti-roll bar will have a dramatic effect on the way your VW handles, the tendency being to put greater loading on the tyres and increase the amount of understeer. This increase will have a tendency to counteract the Beetle's normal oversteer characteristics. To locate the new sway bar, if they are not supplied with it, you should install a set of urethane bushings and new clamps. Do not try to reuse the originals as the chances are the rubber bushes will be worn and the clamps rusted. Finally,

You should note that there were two types of front strut used on the Super Beetles, the early type having a three-bolt mounting on the end of the strut itself. This design was also used on the Type 4 models.

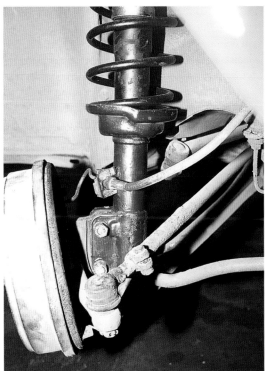

The later design – similar to that used on VW Golfs – relied on a pair of bolts which passed through the side of the strut. This design is easier to adjust for camber. The two designs of strut are not interchangeable.

The best way to drop the front is to install a pair of adjustable short struts. These accept VW Golf GTI damper inserts and have the added benefit of a lower spring cup which can be moved up and down the strut to alter the ride height.

When lowering the front end, the angle of the tie rods changes, resulting in excessive bump steer. This can be overcome by installing a bump steer kit which allows the tie rod ends to be installed from below the steering arms, like this.

although not necessarily essential for improved handling, a new steering damper should be fitted if the old unit shows any sign of leaking or weakness. It is possible to buy uprated dampers from Koni, and other manufacturers, but it is questionable whether there is any major benefit to be gained on a torsion bar Beetle. On MacPherson strut models, the condition of the steering damper can have a serious effect on the way the car drives – as mentioned earlier, these models are susceptible to front end 'shimmies'. Anything you can do to ensure the suspension and steering are exactly as the factory intended is worthwhile.

IMPROVING THE BRAKES
Faster speeds require better brakes!

When you build a Beetle which is capable of exceeding 100mph with ease, something rather more serious is going to have to be done to the braking system than simply ensuring it meets the factory specification. In reality, many fast road cars are grossly under-braked, with the driver relying solely on the disc brakes or, worse still, the drums, which Volkswagen installed when the car was built.

All too often, the brakes are the last thing to get any attention – people will happily spend their life savings on building the motor they always promised themselves, followed soon after by expenditure on a bullet-proof transmission. Only if there is any money left will they think about upgrading the suspension and braking systems to suit. Can you imagine the uproar (and the legal cases) that would follow if a major manufacturer thought that way? Most modern cars have more braking power than

they actually need, but it is far safer to be over-braked than under-braked. Not convinced? Think about it next time you have to perform an emergency stop from high speed….

At the very least, your fast-road car should have factory disc brakes at the front and Type 3 drums at the rear – but this should be considered a minimum. If your car is an early link-pin model then you are in for more expense as there is no factory disc brake set-up for the front end. To begin with, we'll look at the options available to the owner of these pre-'65 cars, few as they are.

Basically, there are two avenues open as far as link-pin Beetles are concerned: installing a set of Porsche 356 drum brakes or an aftermarket disc brake conversion. All Porsche 356s came with king- and link-pin front suspension, which owed much to the Beetle in terms of design. In fact, so close was it in concept that it is possible to substitute all the Porsche parts from the link-pins outwards. In days past, off-road racers in the USA favoured the Porsche 356 spindles over the VW forgings because they were far stronger – and a straight swap. Today, while there are other alternatives available to the off-roader, the possibilities are still there for the fast-road enthusiast.

The beauty of the 356 drum brakes is that they feature huge cast-aluminium drums with cast-iron liners, which measure a full 280mm (or 11ins) in diameter. The friction area is 390sq cm and, while this is not as great as that of a Type 3 drum, the larger diameter makes the brake far more effective. The other great benefit, in terms of efficiency, is that the front brakes are of the twin-leading shoe type – ie, there are two wheel cylinders per brake assembly, resulting in a far greater braking effort.

The 356 brakes came in two styles, those from the 356A having cooling ribs which ran around the circumference of the drum, the later 356B type having radial finning. While the later style is generally believed to be superior, the earlier type was less prone to distortion. Installation of the drums on the front of the car involves either installing the entire brake package, with the stub axle complete with king- and link-pin assemblies, or just the brake backing plates and drums by themselves. While neither is a difficult swap, the former is certainly more straightforward as the latter requires the mixing and matching of wheel bearings to complete.

At the rear, installing the 356 drums is very much a bolt-on operation except that, in some instances, the inside of the brake drum can rub lightly on the springs retaining the brake linings. To combat this, it may be necessary to install a thin spacer between the drum and the bearing retainer to gain a little extra clearance – alternatively, the bearing retainer from a 1950s Beetle can be used.

Fitting a full set of 356 drum brakes will make a tremendous difference to the stopping power of your

Not only was the Type 3 the first VW to come with disc brakes but it also came with larger rear drum brakes, which can be adapted to fit the Beetle. For those operating on a budget, stock front discs with Type 3 rear drums is a good combination.

The Porsche 356A and B models used 11in diameter aluminium drum brakes all round which can be transplanted onto any king- and link-pin Beetle. This 356B rear drum has been redrilled to accept the later Porsche 5-stud wheels.

The beauty of the 356 drum conversion is that it requires no modification to fit onto the Beetle. This is the inner workings of the rear brake assembly showing the large brake shoes and wheel cylinder.

Beetle, especially from speed, where their resistance to fade is far better than the original set-up. They will also accept any Beetle five-lug wheel.

There is, however, a downside to all this: Porsche 356 brake assemblies are becoming increasingly hard to find and, consequently, more expensive to buy. Beware of cheap sets on offer at a swap meet – all too often they have worn or distorted beyond the acceptable limits and cannot be remachined. Also note that 356 brakes can succumb to corrosion between the liner and the aluminium drum, a problem not easy to cure.

The other alternative is to install a set of brakes from a Porsche 356C. These cars came with four-wheel disc brakes, the fronts being a straight swap onto a Beetle just so long as you also use the Porsche stub axle assembly – you'll need this as it incorporates the brake calliper mountings. At the back, the installation is a little more complex as you need to change the axle tubes as well as everything else from thereon out, not forgetting the brake master cylinder. The three drawbacks with using 356C brakes are cost, lack of availability and the fact that you cannot any longer use VW five-lug wheels, as all 356Cs came with the later Porsche small five-bolt stud pattern. However, this does allow the fitment of any of the traditional Fuchs light-alloy wheels from the 911 series without

There are a number of aftermarket rear disc brake conversions available, including this one from the German Car Company in England. The kit comes complete with all fittings and allows the use of the stock handbrake cables.

The CB Performance kit is similar and is also ready to bolt on straight out of the box. New brake cables and pipes are supplied, making this a foolproof installation on any four-bolt wheel Beetle. The difference with rear discs is incredible.

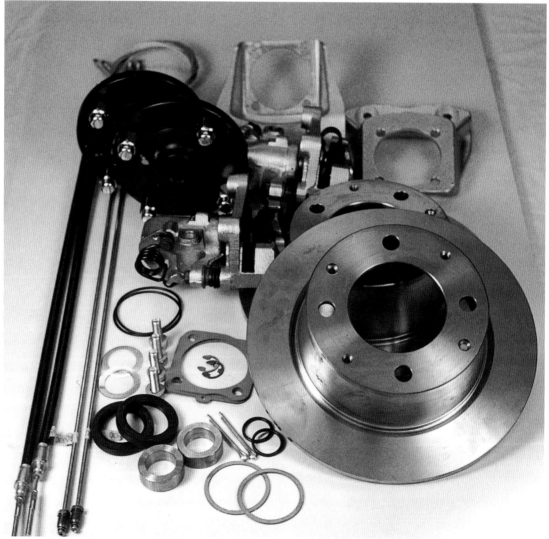

having to use adaptors or redrilling the hubs.

If you have your heart set on a front disc brake conversion which retains the VW 205mm 'wide-five' stud pattern, there are kits available from CNC and Neal in the USA which include discs, callipers and all hardware. Originally developed for use on off-road vehicles, these kits are extremely well engineered and would not look out of place on an out-and-out show vehicle, with billet aluminium callipers and hubs, along with cross-drilled brake discs. In conjunction with Bernard Newbury in the UK, Neal has also developed a pedal assembly to match its brake system which can be installed straight into a Beetle without major surgery. Installation of the disc brake kit simply involves removal of the stock brake and stub-axle assemblies and installing the new components in their place.

Owners of four-bolt models can upgrade the front brakes of their Beetles by installing the callipers from a Talbot Horizon family saloon. These are a straightforward swap and are significantly more powerful than the stock VW calliper, as well as being inexpensive and fairly readily available. At the rear of the car, you can simply fit an aftermarket disc brake conversion. These are available off the shelf from CB Performance and their agents, as well as the German Car Company in the UK. Both kits come complete with new discs, hubs, callipers and mounting brackets and also allow the use of a cable-operated parking brake, a legal requirement in many countries.

These aftermarket kits represent excellent value for money and are the perfect way to upgrade the braking system of a late-model Beetle. There are

further alternatives, such as the installation of Porsche 944 or German Kerscher disc assemblies, both of which will be detailed in the section on all-out street cars.

To recap, a link-pin Beetle can be uprated by the addition of either a full set of Porsche 356 brakes, drum or disc, or by adding aftermarket disc brake conversions, front and rear, from companies such as CB Performance, German Car Company, Neal or CNC. A ball-joint Beetle can benefit from factory front discs, with or without Talbot Horizon callipers, along with one of the above aftermarket rear disc conversions. In all cases, where disc brakes are fitted in place of drums, a matching master cylinder, with residual pressure valve, should be installed.

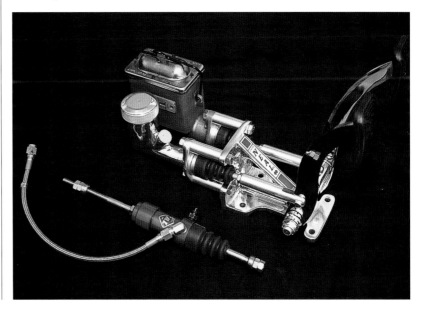

All-out Street

ENGINES FOR ALL-OUT VWs
Stepping ever closer to the magic 200bhp…

The sky really is the limit here, but the matter of what constitutes a street motor is open to debate. While we acknowledge that it is perfectly possible to drive a car fitted with a 260bhp full-race engine on the street, as long as you are prepared to run high-octane race fuel and to rebuild the engine on a semi-regular basis, the kind of engine we shall be considering is one which can be driven on regular pump fuel and won't need to be torn apart every few weeks.

Much of what has already been said concerning a fast road engine holds true, especially as far as the crankcase is concerned. Without wishing to repeat ourselves unnecessarily, do not use anything other than a late-type dual-relief valve case which has been drilled and tapped for a full-flow oiling system. In addition to this, it is highly recommended that the center main bearing saddle be shuffle-pinned to prevent the case halves moving under load at high rpm – these shuffle-pins must be installed by a professional machine shop.

The principal areas where an all-out street engine may differ to one with a fast road specification is in the choice of crankshaft and rods, cylinder heads, camshaft, carburettors and exhaust system. There is, as has been said, no substitute for cubic inches and at this stage the best way to achieve this is by installing a longer stroke crankshaft. An 84mm stroker is an ideal choice for a high-performance street engine as it can be used inside a factory-type crankcase with little problem, as long as the correct type of con-rod is used. Most 84mm cranks will come with the smaller Porsche 53mm rod journals, allowing the use of compact aftermarket rods, thus requiring less clearancing inside the case. There is an added advantage to using the smaller journal, too, in that the crankshaft will be much stronger across the crank webs.

At this stage, especially if some occasional drag racing is envisaged, it is worth considering using a wedge-mated crankshaft and flywheel combination. Wedge-mating is the process whereby the inside of the flywheel is welded up and remachined with a taper to match a similar taper ground on the crankshaft. Once the two are united and the gland nut tightened to 300lbft or more, there is very little chance of the flywheel ever coming loose. Naturally, 8-dowelling is also carried out. Berg, Bugpack and Pauter Machine all list wedge-mated crankshafts amongst their product line, any of which would be perfectly suitable for the task in hand, while both Pauter and Scat also offer flanged crankshafts. However, the latter are not considered necessary for street applications, being primarily intended for use on drag race cars running slicks.

The choice of con-rods open to the engine builder is better now than it has ever been, with several manufacturers offering high-quality forgings which are ideal for our intended purpose. For many years, the industry norm was to use a Porsche 912 con-rod as it was both compact and readily available. However, this has fallen from favour as the 912 rod has also proved to be inherently weak, being prone to breakage at the rod bolt. Another disadvantage is that the 912 rod is too short to be used efficiently with cranks larger than 78mm stroke.

Far better choices are available from Carrillo, Bugpack and Pauter Machine, each of whom produce rods in a variety of lengths and journal sizes to suit almost every application. Of these, the most expensive by far are the Carrillos and because of this many people have chosen to use the similar Bugpack alternative. The author's own 185bhp

street car uses 5.6in Bugpack rods with Porsche journals on an Okrasa 84mm crankshaft.

The question of rod length is sure to cause debate among engine builders, with some feeling that the ratio of rod length (the measurement between the center points of the rod journal and the wrist pin) has little effect on the characteristics of an engine, while others believe the ratio has a fundamental influence on the way an engine produces power. It is generally agreed, however, that a stock-length rod is only suitable for strokes up to 78mm, with longer (typically 5.5in or 5.6in) rods being the best choice with an 82mm or 84mm crank. Certainly longer rods do reduce the side-loading on pistons, which will help to reduce cylinder and piston ring wear, but the down side is that they result in an engine which is far wider than stock. This can cause problems getting the cooling tinware to fit correctly and will also make installation in the engine bay of a stock (especially an early) Beetle something of a chore. Longer rods will result in the power band being moved slightly higher up the rpm range, although on an all-out street engine this may not be critical.

When assembling a new crank and rod combination in a case, even one which has been supplied pre-clearanced for use with a stroker crank, it is important to check that there is adequate space for the crank to turn without the rods – or the crank itself – coming into contact with any part of the crankcase or camshaft. In general, where a stroke of up to 78mm is used, the amount of clearancing that

has to be carried out is relatively minimal. However, with strokes of 84mm and above, there is a need to remove a fair amount more material, with attention having to be paid to the clearance between the crankshaft/rod and the camshaft lobes – this is especially important where a cam with a fairly extreme profile is being used. It is possible to purchase cams which have had the lobes slimmed down slightly to help solve this problem – Gene Berg Enterprises is one company which can supply such products. It is also important to check the side-clearance between the con-rod and the crankshaft. On a hot street engine, this should be between 8 and 10 thou (0.2 - 0.25mm) to allow adequate throughflow of oil past the bearings.

As far as pistons and cylinders are concerned, there has been a move in recent years away from the

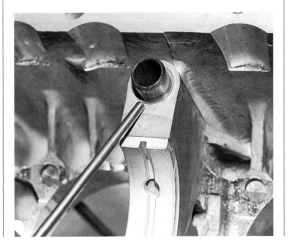

A superb example of a well-presented hot street engine: 48IDA Webers, which have been bored out to 51mm, Vertex magneto, Berg linkage and VW Type 181 fanhousing. Black finish to tinware is attractive and functional.

Shuffle-pinning the crankcase center main bearing studs is a sure way to prevent the case halves moving around at high rpm. Note that this case has also been clearanced for a long stroke crankshaft.

traditional 90.5mm and 92mm bores up to the larger 94mm type. To begin with, these were considered the domain of race engines but there are now many street motors which happily use 94s without problem. Most aftermarket piston and cylinder kits are manufactured by Cima/Mahle and they give excellent service. The only area in which they perhaps need to be improved for high-performance street use is in the choice of piston rings. The stock ductile iron rings are fine but cylinder sealing can be improved by the use of Total Seal or Childs & Albert Z-gap rings which are readily available for both 92mm and 94mm VW pistons.

On the left is a 90.5mm piston (which gives 1776cc with a stock crank) while, by way of comparison, on the right is a 94mm piston (1914cc with 69mm stroke). These are CIMA/Mahle forged pistons with graphite coating.

When it comes to heads, there are many options open to you, including reworking a set of factory castings, such as this 040 head by Adam Wik. Note welding around the inlet port to allow more radical port design.

Viewed in close up, you can see how the stock round ports have been enlarged and reshaped into a kind of rounded 'D'. Although the valve guide bosses have been cut back, the guides themselves have not been shortened.

The pistons supplied with the Cima kits are good quality forgings and, while there was a quality problem a few years ago with 94mm pistons, they appear to give good service on all but the most extreme engines. If there is any doubt about their suitability in the mind of the engine builder, it is possible to substitute aftermarket pistons from Venolia, Wiseco or JE, the main advantage of which is that they are stronger and can be more deeply 'notched' (ie, machined for greater valve clearance) than the Cima type. An engine which runs an 84mm crank and a set of 94mm cylinders will have a capacity of 2332cc – a considerable increase over the stock 1584cc! – yet be perfectly suitable for extended road use.

When it comes to cylinder heads, there are several possibilities available, ranging from welded factory castings to aftermarket products such as Street Eliminators and Superflos (or SF heads as they are now known). The original VW dual-port head can be modified to accept up to 42mm inlet valves without too much problem, along with 37mm exhaust valves. To gain the greatest benefit from these valves, it will be necessary to weld the head adjacent to the inlet ports to allow them to be opened up to improve the air flow. In most cases, this will also mean that the inlet manifolds will have to be welded to suit, so that they can be matched precisely to the new port shape. There are no disadvantages to using welded factory-style heads other than the increased labour costs. For many years, such heads have been the mainstay of the performance industry, at least as far as hot street engines are concerned. Only in relatively recent times have people begun to use aftermarket heads on their street cars, not always with the success they might have hoped for.

The biggest advantage of the aftermarket heads is that they tend to have more material in crucial areas, allowing deeper flycutting, more radical porting and higher valve spring pressures. In between the all-new castings, such as the Street Eliminators, and the factory dual-ports are the 042s and 044s. We won't consider the 041 at this stage as it is really not a suitable head for an all-out street motor. Both the 042s and the 044s can be used to good effect on high-horsepower engines, although they will need extensive reworking if they are to satisfy the demands of a large-capacity engine of 2.2

The exhaust port has been opened up substantially to allow the engine to breathe. Once again, note that although the guide boss has been removed, the guide is untouched. Also note that sufficient material has been left for the exhaust gasket to seal.

Large 42mm x 38mm valves allow even a 2.2-litre engine to breath at high rpm, yet are not so big that bottom end performance suffers unduly. Combustion chambers have been opened out to unshroud valves.

Street Eliminator is a popular aftermarket head for hot street cars, but can cause problems as these heads tend to run hotter than stock castings. Note the cruder fin design compared with a factory head.

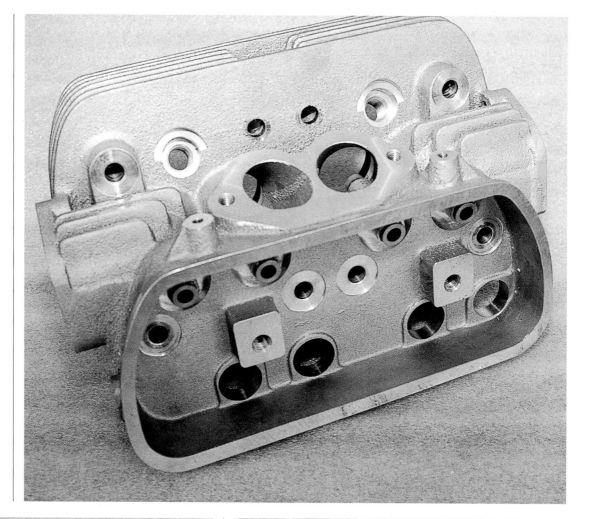

Out of the box, the Street Eliminators offer a lot of potential but you will still need to spend time finishing them properly. Note how ports have not been blended into the valve seats and milled finish of combustion chamber.

litres or more. As might be expected, the area which needs the most attention is the inlet port, which will need to be welded and enlarged if the head is to work on a large-capacity, big-valve engine. Some cylinder head specialists also reweld the sparking plug hole and drill it to accept smaller 12mm plugs, the main aim of which is to allow larger valves to be fitted without increasing the head's vulnerability to cracking between the valve seats and the spark plug.

Pauter Machine's 'B' head is a an excellent example of a welded factory head which is equally at home on a hot street or an all-out race engine. With

Street Eliminator on left has enlarged exhaust port compared with factory head. However, lack of cooling fins round the port is the main cause of this aftermarket head running hotter than the stock head.

the factory cooling fins still in place, this type of head is an ideal candidate for use on a dual-purpose vehicle which sees regular street use and weekend trips to the strip. One of the biggest problems with many of the aftermarket heads is that they tend to run hotter than the originals, the amount of finning cast into the heads being less than that of the

In the foreground is a stock head being readied for extensive reshaping by Pauter Machine. Note the welding above the inlet port. In the background is a finished head with its radically reshaped inlet ports.

Finished Pauter 'B' head (far left) showing the considerable work that has gone into redesigning the inlet port. This amount of reprofiling would not be possible without first adding extra material in the form of aluminium welding.

This head (near left) has been machined to accept 94mm cylinders – note how the flycutting tool has cut into the cylinder head stud holes. This does not represent a problem as the cylinder does not seal against the side of the head, only against the edge of the chamber.

Pauter 'B' head nearing completion – note that spark plug bosses still have to be finished. Heads have been equipped with 42mm x 37mm valves and modified to accept smaller 12mm spark plugs. This reduces the risk of cracking between plug hole and valve seats.

Beware the stock appearance, for Jim Kaforski's sedan packs a 200bhp punch, which allows it to trip the quarter-mile timing lights in just 12.7 seconds! The car epitomises what an all-out street car is all about: performance without compromise!

For optimum power output, it is vital that all combustion chambers are of equal volume – this means checking each of them with a burette and a liquid, such as paraffin. The head shown is an Auto-craft 910 race head.

original VW castings. When heads run hot, there is an increased risk of cracks appearing, valve seats moving (or dropping out altogether) and detonation. However, with proper attention paid to the cooling system and with compression ratios kept to a sensible level, it is possible to make aftermarket heads, such as the Street Eliminator type, live on a street engine, although it is not recommended that they be used where the car sees regular, long freeway journeys.

As we stated at the beginning of this section, the sky really is the limit – it all depends on what you expect from your car. Although everyone will tell you that it is not possible to use Superflo (SF) heads on the street (they tend to run far hotter than a stock-type head), there are several cars which run them without problem, although these can hardly be termed daily drivers. Similarly when it comes to the matter of compression ratios, as a general rule, it

Superflo – or S/F – heads may be used on a street engine as long as due regard is given to cooling as they are primarily designed for race use. Note oval Cosworth-style inlet ports and wide three-bolt manifold fixing.

is best to stay under 9.5:1 on an engine which has to be used regularly. However, that does not mean that there are not street-legal VWs running with as much as 12:1 compression ratios (or more!) but let us just say that if you don't mind using race fuel in place of the regular pump gas, then almost anything is possible.

To keep things in some kind of perspective, 9.0:1 is a respectable compression ratio to run on the street without having too many problems with poor fuel – most aftermarket heads these days can be used with unleaded fuel, the quality of which tends to be far superior to the last remaining leaded fuel still available, although for how much longer remains to be seen. To a certain degree, a high compression ratio can be compensated for by using a cam with long duration – the longer the valve is open, the more compression pressure is allowed to 'bleed off' at low rpm, effectively reducing the compression ratio. If a high CR is used on an engine with a low-lift, short-duration camshaft, the cylinder pressure will build up far earlier in the cycle, resulting in detonation problems and overheating. Looking at things from the reverse point of view, to work at its most efficient, a high-lift, long-duration camshaft needs to be used with a high CR, otherwise the engine will feel 'soft' and lack any mid-range power.

On the matter of valve sizes, the larger the engine, the more it will benefit from an increase in valve diameter. In general, an all-out street engine

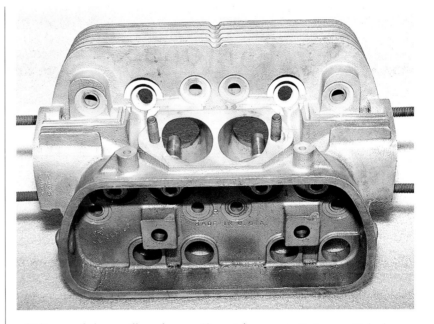

Performance Technology head based on a JC Performance casting shows enlarged inlet ports. Note use of 12mm plugs and minimal finning around exhaust port. JC head castings are no longer available.

of 2 litres and above will need to use 42mm inlet and 37mm exhaust valves at the very least. Increase the capacity to 2.2 litres and the inlet valve could be increased to 44mm with a 38mm exhaust. It is not unheard of for 48mm x 40mm combinations to be used (with aftermarket heads) on street-legal VWs which only see occasional road use. One problem which does arise as valve sizes increase and engine rpm rises is valve float due to the increased weight of the valve train. Racers get round this by using titanium valves and retainers but on the road

the best all-round choice is a set of stainless steel valves used with titanium retainers. You will need to install good-quality dual valve springs, with Vasco-Jet, K-Motion, Berg or similar being a good choice for a radical street motor. As with all dual springs, the valve guide bosses on factory heads will have to be cut to accept them, although most aftermarket castings will come pre-machined to accept dual springs.

Be aware that the larger the valve size and the bigger the ports, the less flexible the engine will become, especially if used in conjunction with a radical camshaft profile, 48IDA Webers and a large-diameter exhaust system. The more outrageous your engine combination, the less pleasant it will become to drive in traffic. However, if that is of no concern to you, then be prepared to have a wild ride when you slam that throttle wide open!

If flexibility and good fuel economy are not prime considerations – and, to some extent, they have to take a back seat when building an all-out street motor – then the choice of camshafts is wide open. There are so many cams available (in the *Aircooled VW Engine Interchange Manual* we list over 200!) that it is not possible to be too specific about recommendations, but it is important to acknowledge the fact that all high-performance camshafts will increase top-end power at the expense of bottom-end output. This is a fact of life which cannot be ignored – you cannot 'take' without 'giving' something in return. In general, simply increasing the valve lift will not greatly affect

Lash caps are used to prevent the tips of the valve stems wearing, especially where high-lift, long duration camshafts are used. The caps simply slip on top of the valve. They are available in various thicknesses to allow for variations in rocker arm geometry.

From the left: stock valve spring is a single winding; heavy-duty single spring is suitable for engines with mild cam profile that are used at low rpm; heavy-duty dual springs are for high-rpm motors; Vasco dual springs are for all-out high-rpm applications.

the lower rpm power but will help to increase torque and high-end rpm, assuming the cylinder heads can flow the extra mixture OK. If the heads cannot cope with the increased demands, then flexibility across the rpm range will suffer. Simply fitting a high-lift cam to an otherwise stock engine is not the answer. Increasing camshaft duration will push the power band higher up the rpm range at the expense of bottom-end power. Long duration and low rpm do not go together.

Nowadays, the trend is to use what a few years ago would have been considered race cams on a hot street motor. Grinds such as Engle's FK-87 are popular, offering 320° of duration and 0.390in of lift at the cam (approximately 0.580in at the valve with 1.5:1 ratio rockers). In a large capacity engine of 2.1 litres or more, a cam such as this will prove to be perfectly acceptable, providing the cylinder heads and induction systems have been modified accordingly. The author's 2160cc (84mm x 90.5mm) street car runs an FK-87 with 42mm x 37mm valves, 48IDAs and a modest 8.5:1 compression ratio. The end result is a car which can be driven around town at 30mph in fourth gear (on a close-ratio transmission) and yet return low-13 second passes on street tyres at the strip. In general, the larger the engine, the more radical the cam specification you can get away with, especially if the extra capacity has been gained by the use of a stroker crank. The longer the crank, the more bottom end torque, hence the ability to use a long-duration cam.

Where outright performance is the main objective, with driveability taking something of a back seat, the use of 48IDA Webers has almost become de rigueur. These carbs have been the number one choice on hot street VWs and drag race

Valve retainers – from left: stock pressed steel is only acceptable for mild applications; chrome-moly retainer is for use with heavy-duty valve springs; titanium retainers help reduce valve train weight and are necessary for high-rpm use.

Stock cam gear on left has teeth cut on a helix to reduce noise, but this can cause the thrust face of the cam bearings to wear prematurely when used with stronger valve springs. Straight-cut gears (right) solve this problem but are considerably noisier.

Dual 48IDA Webers have been the number one choice for racers and hot street use for many years. The carburettor was originally designed for use on Ford V8 engines in race applications but soon proved ideal for use on large displacement VW motors.

The 48IDA can be bored out to 51mm and fitted with larger throttle butterflies using kits from Berg or JayCee Enterprises. This engine is also fitted with larger inlet manifolds to allow correct matching to both carburettors and inlet ports.

It is vital that you run a fuel pressure regulator to prevent the carburettors from flooding, especially at low rpm. This Holley unit also doubles as a T-piece, splitting the fuel flow to both carburettors. Note rigid aluminium fuel line and braided hoses.

cars for almost 30 years. While they may not have the finesse of modern carburettors like the 48mm Dell'Orto DRLA, 48IDAs are guaranteed to deliver the horsepower with the maximum efficiency. On engines over 2.3 litres, it may be worth considering having the 48s bored out to 51mm, this conversion being available from Gene Berg Enterprises and JayCee Enterprises in the USA. The major drawback of any IDA-derived carburettor is that the progression circuit is not too sophisticated, meaning that in everyday driving they can suffer from flat

By far the best way to set up a performance engine is to run it on a dynamometer. That way the engine can be run under load and the fuel system optimized for maximum power delivery. Both power output and torque can be measured across the rpm range.

Dick Landy Industries manufactures this impressive supercharger system for the VW engine – about which great claims are made. B&M supercharger is used on purpose-built manifold. Either Holley or Dell'Orto carburettor can be used.

spots just off idle. However, when correctly set up on a large capacity engine, they can be made to work extremely well and, indeed, it is possible to have new progression circuits drilled in your IDAs to help overcome the problem. There can be no real recommendation made as to how the carbs should be set up, as this is something that has to be carried out on a dyno or rolling road. A ball-park jetting choice can be made following our formula at the end of the chapter.

There are other induction systems for an all-out street engine: turbocharging, fuel-injection or supercharging, although it has to be said the the latter is not widely accepted as a means of extracting the maximum power from a VW engine. Dick Landy Industries manufactures a VW-only supercharger set-up which is aimed at both the street and off-road markets, but it is not a popular conversion and only rarely seen. Turbo systems are available off the shelf from CB Performance in the USA, with the kits comprising a blow-through set-up based around single or dual Dell'Orto DRLA carburettors. High on street 'cred', these turbo systems have been developed to a point where there need be no concern about long-term reliability, just so long as the rest of the engine is in good health.

What were once considered race-only set-ups, which usually consist of a large single Dell'Orto side-draught DHLA or Holley four-barrel carburettor used as part of a draw-through system, offer tremendous horsepower potential for the street racer but can result in poor driveability if badly

conceived. Needless to say, reliability can suffer too if the system is not properly engineered. However, experienced companies such as Kawell Racing Engines in Tennessee have built many draw-through turbo systems over the years, several of which have seen regular use on the street without any problems. If boost pressure is kept within reason (7-8psi, or 0.5 bar), a well-built turbocharged engine can live to see a high mileage without drama, although you should be aware that turbo systems which are designed to produce high levels of horsepower (200+bhp) will almost certainly require the use of high-octane race fuel.

Much pioneering work on fuel-injection systems has been carried out in the USA by companies such as Gene Berg Enterprises and CB Performance, and latterly in the UK by DTA, in conjunction with John Maher Racing. CB Performance's system is not a fully mapped design, lacking the ability to control the ignition system. It also comes pre-programmed to suit specific engine combinations. The Haltech system from Gene Berg is more user friendly in that it is possible to map the fuel and ignition systems to suit virtually any engine set-up. The DTA system claims to be more sophisticated, using more advanced electronics in the search for even greater 'programmability' to allow it to be used with what might be considered extreme engine specifications without loss of driveability.

It is hard to argue against the use of a programmable fuel-injection system when you consider all the advantages over a relatively unsophisticated induction system based around dual 48IDA Webers. While a 48IDA can be set up to run well at idle and also at wide-open throttle, there is precious little control over the mid-throttle settings. Add a radical camshaft and large valves to the equation and driveability can suffer dramatically. The benefit of a fully-programmable fuel-injection system is that, in theory, you can run big-valve heads, a long-duration camshaft and large throttle bodies yet still be able to open the throttle wide at low rpm without having the engine cough and splutter in protest. The ECU (Electronic Control Unit) which controls the injection system will automatically alter the fuel delivery and ignition timing to match the demands being made upon the engine. It is rather like having someone constantly rejetting your carburettors and adjusting the distributor while you drive.

As far as exhaust systems for large capacity engines are concerned, there is no alternative but to use a good-quality merged system measuring at least 1.75in diameter. This should be used in conjunction with, at the very least, a dual quiet muffler set-up or, preferably, a V8-style 'turbo' muffler. The latter is the chosen style amongst those in the know, as the big turbo mufflers offer minimal restriction with the maximum of silencing. The main problem with using such a muffler on a VW is where to locate it. If you don't object to a bulky muffler hanging in full view under the rear valance, then no problem. If your car doesn't run bumpers then you may run into problems with the law, who might take exception to this heat source being on open display. An alternative is to tuck the muffler up under the right-hand bank of cylinders, with the exhaust pipe doubling back under the car once it leaves the collector. This results in a slightly heavier, less efficient system but it does look more appealing and is definitely less likely to result in a traffic ticket! Be aware that some merged header systems will result in your having to cut the rear valance to clear the collector. It is better to find this out before you paint the car rather than having to take a jig-saw to your freshly-painted bodywork when you come to install the engine…

Now for a look at the ignition and fuel systems. While a 009 distributor and coil may be acceptable for a milder engine, our all-out street motor will demand more. At the very least you should fit an aftermarket electronic system, such as the excellent Stinger set-up offered by Gene Berg, but many people favour the MSD 6-AL system which can be used with points or a magnetic triggering set-up. The beauty of the MSD system is that there are many extra 'plug-ins' available, such as spark retard, rev-limiter and shift-light facilities.

For a visual show of intent, there is little to beat a Vertex magneto which has for a long time been the racer's number one choice of ignition. Only in recent times has the magneto given way to the MSD 7-AL race ignition system, although this is not suitable for street use. The beauty of the Vertex is that it produces a fat spark at low rpm, independent of the car's electrical system. The technology may be old (magnetos have been around for almost as long as the internal combustion engine) but it has proved itself over and over again. However, if you wish to add a rev-limiting facility (a must on a high-rpm engine) then you will need to buy a control box, such as Autometer's Pro-Control, which has a dial-in rpm facility. We suggest you use two Pro-Controls with your magneto: one as a rev limiter, the other as a shift-light control.

As for MSD's line of products, the 6-AL system is considered to be the perfect package for the all-out street motor, offering the opportunity to add a rev-limiter, shift-light and other functions, all of which are available from the same company. The 6-AL can be used either with a modified VW distributor, or MSD's own 'billet' unit. Either will work fine, although the MSD distributor is a better engineered (and more modern) design. Magneto or MSD: the choice is yours…

Regarding the fuel system, a high-horsepower, high-rpm engine will make serious demands on the fuel pump and lines. At the very least, you should run a Holley 'Red' pump with a matching regulator, large-diameter fuel lines (-6 minimum or preferably -8) and a vent on the tank. You may wish to install a 'Blue' pump instead, but this must still be used with a 'Red' regulator in order to reduce the fuel pressure to a level acceptable to IDA carburettors. As for fuel itself, use the best quality, highest octane you can get hold of – in the USA, where gas quality is low, that just might mean a high-octane race fuel, such as VP Racing's C-12.

The Vertex magneto (above left) has been around since the 1930s and has been regularly used on hot VW engines since the 1960s. Magnetos generate their own spark independently of the battery. A clamp needs to be used to support the magneto on the crankcase.

DTA fuel-injection system (above) has been developed for use on VW engines by John Maher Racing in the UK. System is fully programmable, with the fuel delivery adjustable by plugging the electronic control unit into a lap-top computer.

Finally, it is also possible to run a full nitrous oxide injection system on a street car, kits being readily available from suppliers such as Nitrous Oxide Systems in California. Nitrous oxide, when injected into the inlet manifold, allows the engine to burn more fuel – more fuel burnt means more power produced. The skill in setting up a nitrous system comes in establishing the correct nitrous/fuel ratio – inject neat nitrous oxide into an engine by itself and, because it releases oxygen when heated, the result will be an excessively lean condition in the combustion chamber. To complement the

An alternative to the magneto on a high-performance engine is the MSD 6-AL ignition system, shown here complete with MSD Blaster coil and billet distributor. Super-clean engine installation uses factory-style hosing on crankcase breathers.

nitrous, you need to inject extra fuel into the engine at the same time.

Nitrous is stored in liquid form in a pressurized bottle, while the extra fuel is provided by a secondary fuel system run from the main tank, consisting of a second electric fuel pump and separate fuel lines. The flow of the nitrous and fuel

The stock transmission
casing can – and will –
break when subjected to
extreme use on the strip. It
usually fails by cracking
across the drain plug.
Welding magnesium gussets
on the underside of the
casing solves this problem.

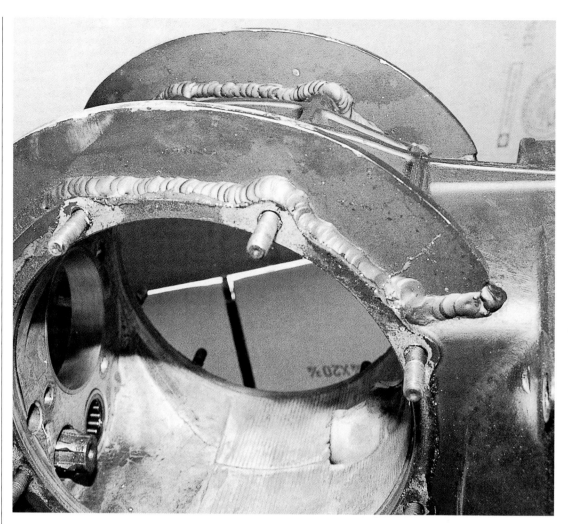

are controlled by two electrically-operated solenoid valves which are set to open at wide-open throttle by way of a micro-switch on the throttle linkage. From the solenoids, the nitrous and fuel are injected into the engine via small brass jets, which are usually located in the inlet manifolds close to the cylinder heads.

By altering the size of the jets, it is possible to vary the power increase available – most basic nitrous kits come with jets which offer a 40bhp increase, but it is possible to achieve as much as 150bhp, or more, on a well-engineered system (and with a well-prepared engine!). Used sparingly, nitrous oxide injection is an excellent way to produce a dual-purpose street/strip engine package.

A well-built all-out street engine need not be the undriveable beast you might think. As long as you avoid extreme camshaft specifications, valve sizes over 42mm x 37mm and a compression ratio of more than 9.0:1, there is no reason on earth why a 2.3-litre engine with 48IDAs and a 185-190bhp power output cannot be driven on a semi-regular basis. The biggest problem you are likely to encounter is a marked decrease in valve guide life, as the combination of heavy valve springs and high cam lift will tend to increase the side-loading on the valve stems, resulting in extra wear. Be aware that worn valve guides ultimately lead to dropped valves,

so be prepared to check them every few thousand miles – yes, that does mean dropping the engine and stripping the top end, but that is a small price to pay for increased reliability.

A recommendation for an all-out street motor? Try an 84mm wedge-mated crank and flywheel assembly, Bugpack or Pauter Machine chrome-moly 5.6in con-rods, 94mm Cima/Mahle cylinders and pistons, Total Seal rings, welded 044 or Street Eliminator heads with 42mm x 37mm valves, 9.0:1 compression, Engle FK-87 camshaft, dual 48IDA Webers and a 1.75in merged exhaust system exiting through a turbo muffler. Correctly set up, this package should be capable of delivering close to 190bhp reliably.

HEAVY-DUTY TRANSMISSIONS
Close-ratio gears and limited slip diffs

When asking for anything up to four times the anticipated power output to pass through the transmission, it is not unreasonable to expect failures to occur. There is simply no way that an original gearbox is going to live with 180 or more horsepower, especially as people don't build high-horsepower engines to treat them gently. At the very least, it will be necessary to uprate the transmission and drivetrain as described in the fast

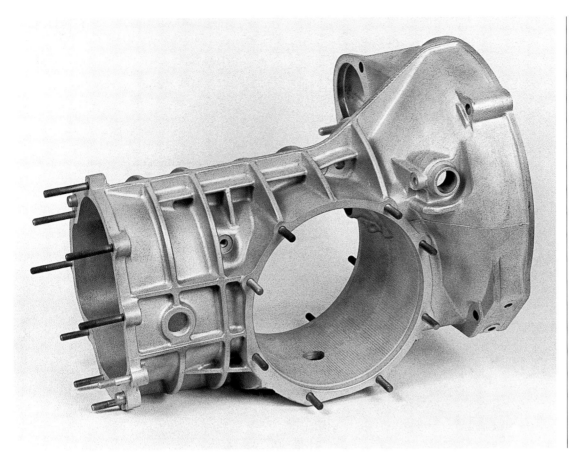

The so-called Rhino case is produced in South America by the VW factory. It is used by many people who feel that it is far stronger than a regular VW transmission casing. However, even a Rhino case will break across the underside.

On the left in the picture below is a Rhino case, while on the right is a conventional case. The extra finning of the former is immediately obvious. In all other respects, the two cases are identical and completely interchangeable.

One weak point of the stock VW gearbox is the pinion bearing support, which can flex and allow the pinion shaft to move in the case. JayCee Enterprises manufactures this chrome-moly replacement (shown on the left) to solve the problem.

road chapter. This will give you a fighting chance of survival but won't allow you to make full use of your new-found horsepower without the prospect of failure looming large in the rear view mirror.

There is still the matter of establishing what kind of use you are intending to put your car through: are you a weekend warrior who likes to flex his Bug's muscles at the strip, or do you prefer to cruise at 100+mph and out-accelerate Porsches on the freeway? Both require horsepower but demand different approaches to the treatment of the transmission. The former will require something more akin to a drag racer's gearbox set-up, while a Porsche or Berg 5-speed will probably be the answer for the latter.

Looking at the street/strip set-up first of all, we'll begin by looking at the transmission casing itself. The original factory casting is superb, being made of a magnesium alloy which is both light and very strong. In most instances, it is perfectly satisfactory as it is but can distort when subjected to violent

Probably the ultimate in transmission casings is the impressive aftermarket casting from Auto-Craft in the USA. Designed to overcome all the problems normally experienced by people using the stock-type transmission, it is as near bullet-proof as is possible.

Despite its race-car looks, the author's roof-chopped '65 sedan is street legal. Swap the road tyres for slicks and unbolt the muffffler and it's time to go racing. 2.1-litre engine carries full cooling and charging system.

Greg Brinton's '67 Beetle runs on race fuel, has a compression ratio of 12.5:1 and develops 217bhp through the muffler! With its Gene Berg 5-speed transmission, this is a car which can still be driven on the freeway.

startline launches on a regular basis. This distortion occurs when the ring and pinion try to separate themselves, pushing the pinion shaft into the 'box while forcing the crown-wheel out to the side. In lower horsepower applications, a heavy-duty side-plate will usually solve this but not so in a high-bhp situation. As the ring and pinion wrestle with each other, the box tries to flex dramatically, eventually cracking across the bottom of the case at its weakest point: the gearbox drain plug. The result is a scrap casing and a wrecked ring and pinion – or possible worse.

To prevent this happening, the most common solution is to weld strengthening gussets along the underside of the casing, on either side of the drain plug. Cut from sheets of magnesium, these have to be welded to the casing in controlled conditions, a task best performed by a specialist in this field. In nine cases out of ten, adding these gussets will cure any potential problems with the casing before they can occur.

A popular alternative is to use the so-called Rhino case – a factory-made gearbox case which features extra strengthening ribs for greater rigidity. Produced in South America, the Rhino case has

proved popular as it is seen as being a cost-effective way to create a stronger driveline However, racers know that you will still need to add gussets to a Rhino case as even they are known to break across the drain plug area. It has also been suggested that these cases are cast from a slightly softer material, meaning that they do not last as long as a stock-type transmission case.

To help prevent the pinion-shaft bearing from moving in the casing, you will need to install an aftermarket chrome-moly type, manufactured by JayCee Enterprises in the USA. This simple

Auto-Craft casing built up into complete transmission. The bellhousing is a separate casting which is bolted onto main casing. Intermediate housing is a new casting but the stock factory nose-cone is retained.

modification prevents the bearing from coming loose in the casing, a problem which will destroy the bearings and eventually lead to the case having to be scrapped. In fact, after a transmission failure of any kind, one of the sure ways to check if the casing is salvageable is to see if the pinion bearing is still a tight interference fit in the case – if it is loose, the case is beyond further use.

The ultimate aftermarket transmission casing for the Type 1 gearbox is that made by Auto-Craft. It is hard to conceive a street car needing such a bullet-proof casing but, there again, there was a time, not long ago, when 200bhp VW engines were the sole domain of the drag racer. The Auto-Craft transmission case is substantial in the extreme and is designed to cure all known shortcomings of the factory casting. It is made from high-strength aluminium and features extensive strengthening both inside and out. It is a two-piece design, the bell-housing being a separate component from the main body of the transmission.

Internally, the greatest weakness is going to be the stock mainshaft, with first and second gears being prone to breakage when subjected to regular abuse. There is a range of alternative mainshafts manufactured by FTC in the USA, offering a number of ratios to cover various applications. Those currently available are as follows:

1st Gear	2nd Gear	1st Gear	2nd Gear
4.11	2.47	3.30	1.93
3.78	2.35	3.10	2.47
3.78	2.21	3.10	2.35
3.55	2.47	3.10	2.21
3.55	2.35	3.10	1.93
3.55	2.21	3.10	1.86
3.55	2.06	3.10	1.59
3.55	1.93	2.91	2.47
3.40	2.21	2.91	2.21
3.30	2.47	2.91	2.06
3.30	2.06	2.58	1.86

Of these, the ones which will be of most relevance to our chosen field are those with the 3.78, 3.55 or 3.40 1st gear. The 4.11 is a popular choice for use in heavy drag race cars, but is far too low for use on the street. Mainshafts with 3.30 and numerically lower 1st gear sets are primarily designed for use in very light vehicles such as sand rails. These heavy-duty mainshafts are all but indestructible, even under the most severe conditions.

Early-style factory mainshafts were located with a snap-ring, while the later type used a thread and matching nut. Both types are interchangeable but all aftermarket mainshafts are made in the late style.

For the remaining 3rd and 4th ratios, there is a

FTC mainshaft in foreground is far stronger than the stock shaft, with heavier teeth cut on a shallow helix. This is a 4.11 1st gear with 2.47 2nd. Note how the teeth of the low 1st gear have had to be cut into the shaft..

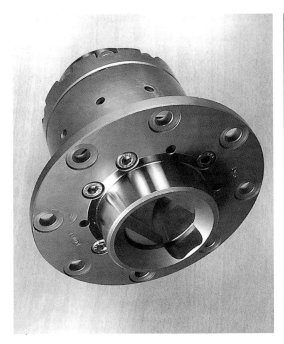

New limited slip differential unit for swing-axle VWs has been developed by Quaife Engineering in England exclusively for Autocavan Volksport. The unit should answer the prayers of all those who lament the passing of the renowned ZF differential.

choice between regular and heavy-duty gear sets. In most instances, the former are fine for road use, offering adequate robustness for most situations with little cause for concern. However, where an engine produces closer to 200bhp it is worth opting for the heavy-duty gear sets. The major difference between the two styles is in the way in which the gear teeth are machined. The regular type has the teeth cut on a sharp helix (the angle of the teeth on the gear is referred to as the 'helix' – the sharper the angle, the weaker the gear) which offers quieter operation, whereas the shallow helix of the heavy-duty gears makes the transmission far stronger but very noisy.

This may not be a problem but is something to consider if your car is to be used for long journeys. Incidentally, early split-case gearboxes had virtually straight-cut first and second gears, giving rise to the familiar whine from the transmission as a split-window Bug is driven away from rest. In addition to installing the new ratios, you will need to weld the synchro hubs as described in the previous chapter on fast-road cars.

In the majority of instances there will be little option but to install a Super-Diff in the transmission of an all-out street car. However, the ideal is to locate (if you can) one of the original ZF limited slip differentials (LSDs) manufactured by the German company until the 1970s. Two designs have been used over the years, one using friction plates, the other a pawl arrangement. It is the latter design which is of interest to us as it is better able to cope with high horsepower levels. It is still possible to purchase a new IRS limited slip diff for a Beetle, but the swing-axle variety is virtually impossible to find new. Good used ones do turn up on occasion but their price is high. The great advantage of the ZF is that it is strong and, being an LSD, transmits the power to both rear wheels equally. This puts an end to one-wheel burnouts and erratic startline launches, as well as preventing the inside rear wheel from wanting to spin as you accelerate hard out of a sharp corner. In all but the most extreme situations, the ZF has proved to be virtually indestructible, capable of handling in excess of 200bhp without problem. Sadly, their rarity makes them something of a luxury nowadays.

There may be light at the end of the tunnel,

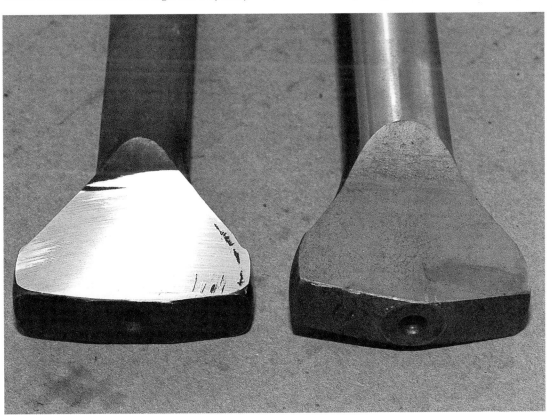

Stock axle on left won't withstand too much abuse from a high-horsepower engine, especially when the car is taken to the drag strip. Aftermarket axle on right is far stronger – note the thicker shaft. Race axles are available to fit all swing-axle Beetles.

For many enthusiasts, installing a Porsche 5-speed transmission from a 911 is the ultimate, the five close-ratio gears offering the best of both worlds: excellent acceleration and good freeway cruising. Unit requires fabrication of a new cross-member.

From below, it is possible to see how the Porsche gear selector housing is located lower than that of the Beetle. This means that the chassis has to be cut to allow the gear linkage to hook up to the transmission.

though, in the form of a new swing-axle LSD unit made exclusively for Autocavan Volksport in England by leading transmission specialists, Quaife Engineering. A development of Quaife's well-proven LSD unit used in a variety of other makes of car, the new Autocavan component looks set to become the answer to many people's prayers, offering the robustness of the ZF unit at a far lower price. And, of course, it has the added advantage of being available new, off the shelf.

With the case strengthened, an aftermarket mainshaft, heavy-duty gear sets and an unbreakable differential, what's next in line to break? Well, probably one of two things: the ring and pinion or the axles. In truth, the factory ring and pinion assembly is not likely to fail as long as street tyres are used, but if slicks are fitted for occasional strip use then this is a good possibility. The strongest factory ring and pinion is the 3.88:1 unit, followed by the 4.125:1 and then the 4.375:1 ratios. The

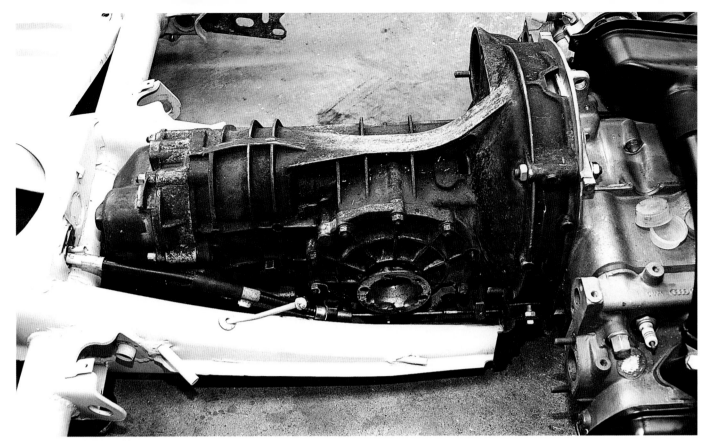

Installation of the Porsche transmission requires the use of an IRS floorpan, or an adapted swing-axle chassis. Note routing of clutch release cable compared with the stock VW transmission. Frame forks need to be modified to clear output flanges.

As the Porsche gearbox uses a different gearchange pattern, the gear lever assembly from the 911 needs to be transplanted into the Beetle as well. The gear linkage itself needs to be cut and shut to marry up with the lever.

3.88:1 is a popular choice among people racing turbocharged cars as it can withstand a lot of abuse. However, in some markets, 3.88 ring and pinions are hard to find. For this reason, the 4.125 has proved to be the most popular, being widely available and more than strong enough for most situations.

Axles are another matter: the stock axles won't last if you intend making full use of the available horsepower. There is a variety of axles on offer in short (pre-'67), long with short brake-drum spline (1967 only) and long with long spline ('68-on) styles. Short axles measure 26.75in in overall length, while the longer styles measure 27.75in. Installation is basically a matter of removing the old axle and replacing it with the new, although you may need to change the fulcrum plates in the differential side gears of a swing-axle transmission to match the dimensions of the new axle. Once installed, you will never need to worry about the

Gene Berg 5-speed conversion of the VW transmission features this extended pinion shaft to allow fitment of the extra gear. Mainshaft is similarly extended. You can either have your own shafts modified or purchase new ones outright from Gene Berg Enterprises.

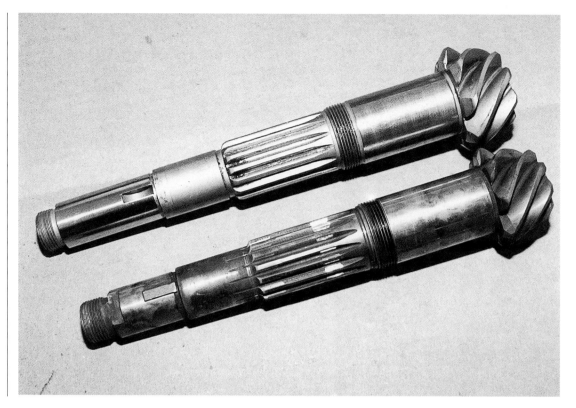

Berg conversion also includes this special intermediate housing which places the new 5th gear on the outside of the casing – this is the same principle used by Porsche on the 911 and VW on the late-type vans.

axles again as it unlikely you will ever break an aftermarket shaft.

IRS transmissions are another matter as it is necessary to spend rather a lot of money in order to make one bullet-proof. Even when a ZF LSD is installed, there is no guarantee that you won't break something in this vital area as the output shafts of the ZF unit can still fail like those of a stock diff. The weakest links in the IRS chain are the output shafts, the CV joints and the axles themselves,

although the latter are not normally a major problem area on a street car. To strengthen these potential weaknesses, you should consider installing aftermarket output flanges which accept Type 2 or Porsche 930 CV joints. However, this does not cure the problem of weak output shafts, which will still be prone to failure at the base of the splines. Unfortunately, due to the relative lack of interest in the IRS unit, there has been little development of new products to solve this inherent problem.

The Type 2 and Porsche CV joints are far more robust than the stock type, but require the use of matching axles. Currently, the majority of aftermarket axles are designed for use with the Porsche CVs, those available from Dura Blue being available in various lengths to suit different applications. To further strengthen the CV joints, Dura Blue also offers chrome-moly bearing cages and axle boot flanges. The matching output flanges are only available splined to match the late-type Type 2 IRS transmissions. With a full range of Dura Blue flanges, modified Porsche CV joints and Dura Blue axles, the author successfully campaigned his 420bhp turbocharged sedan for four years without a single failure, proof indeed that IRS transmissions can be made to work.

One of the most frustrating aspects of having a well-built fast street car is that, to make the most of the engine's powerband, you need to run close-ratio gears which, in turn, tend to make long-distance travel something of a chore. The solution could be to install either a Porsche or Berg 5-speed transmission. The former is better suited to vehicles which are intended for use more as freeway cruisers than out-and-out street and strip cars as it is not as

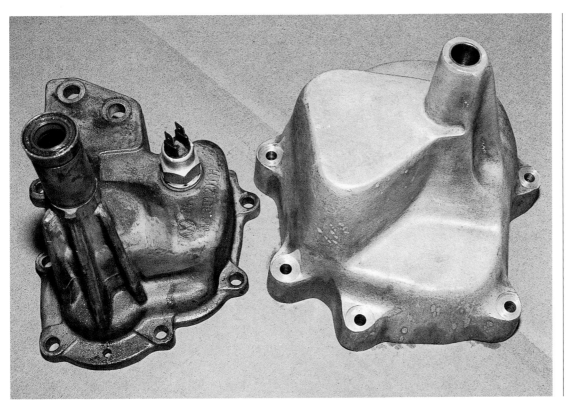

strong as you might at first expect. In fact, drag racers in the past who have experimented with using Porsche 5-speed 'boxes have discovered that it is not unknown for the pinion shaft to break all too easily. However, the Porsche gearbox is a beautifully engineered unit which is available with a variety of ratio and final drives. Unfortunately, it is also only available as an IRS unit, making it unsuitable for use in an early-style swing-axle Beetle.

Installation of the Porsche trans in a Beetle requires a reasonable amount of modification to the floorpan, principally consisting of the fabrication of new mountings to support the front end of the transmission and modifying the gear linkage. If the 911/01-type Porsche trans is used, the rear (bellhousing) mountings from a Beetle can be installed once part of the original Porsche mountings have been cut off the casing. You will also need to modify the clutch release mechanism so that you can install the VW release bearing, allowing a regular Beetle clutch to be used. Furthermore, the CV joints will foul the chassis either side of the gearbox, a minor problem which can be overcome with the judicious use of a ball-peen hammer.

Inside the car, the gear-shift assembly from the Porsche will also have to be used, as the stock VW lever cannot be used with the conversion, requiring a certain amount of surgery to the tunnel of the Beetle's chassis. Fortunately, the Porsche gear-linkage rod can be used, although it needs to be lengthened by around 6ins.

The beauty of the Porsche 5-speed conversion is that used 911 transmissions are plentiful and priced surprisingly reasonably, considering their origins.

They offer fairly close ratios with an over-drive fifth gear, which is particularly well-suited to lengthy freeway journeys. In Germany, such conversions are very popular among those who wish to exploit the country's speed-limit-free autobahns to the full.

The alternative to the Porsche unit is the ingenious Berg 5-speed assembly, which is based on the Type 1 transmission. This has the advantages of requiring far less work to install in a Beetle as well as being available for both swing-axle and IRS vehicles. It allows the use of ultra-close first-through-fourth gears to be used with a stock-ratio

The simplest way to solid mount a transmission is to install one of these inexpensive three-piece kits. However, they do not give adequate support to the frame forks and can lead to the transmission casing cracking at the bellhousing. Install the more rigid cradle type instead.

The Berg weld-in front mounting is the most popular solid front mounting used today. It welds across the underside of the frame forks and bolts to the lower four mounting studs on the intermediate housing. Simple, but very effective.

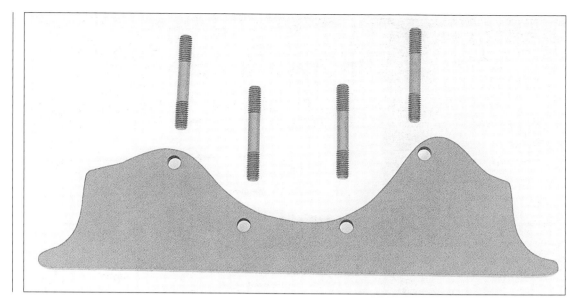

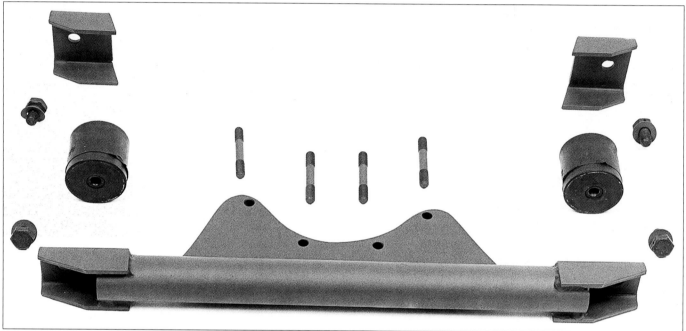

The best compromise for high-performance street cars which require rigid transmission location without too much noise transfer to the inside of the vehicle is to use the Berg 'Super-Duty' rubber-mounted transmission support.

top. This way, you can have your cake and eat it, enjoying the benefits of an all-out race-style trans, with a low fourth gear, yet still retain the ability to cruise on the freeway as if using a stock gearbox.

The conversion consists of lengthened main and pinion shafts, a special intermediate housing, a new nose-cone, extra thrust washers, keys, pinion and mainshaft nuts and all other hardware necessary to complete the transformation from four-speed to five. No specially-made gear ratios are required as the Berg unit uses regular close-ratio or stock factory gear sets, including the extra fifth gear, which is in fact a regular Beetle fourth gear.

The Berg conversion was unavailable for many years due to the relatively small demand – it was probably a case of a great product being available too soon, as it seems in retrospect that the market wasn't yet ready for such an idea. Even today, Berg 5-speeds are relatively uncommon, largely because of the cost of building a full-on close-ratio set-up,

but as people become more aware of the advantages, this situation is sure to change. After all, how else can you run a 3.78 1st, 2.06 2nd, 1.56 3rd and a 1.19 4th gear on a 4.125 ring and pinion and still be able to cruise at 90mph without wringing the engine out too far? Slip into that 0.82 5th gear and long-legged cruising becomes a reality.

Installation in the car is straightforward, with only minor modifications needed to clear the slightly more bulky nose-cone. You need to install a special Berg-manufactured gear shifter on which, to engage fifth gear, you push a button before moving the lever to the right and forward. No other alterations are required.

On the subject of mounting a transmission in an all-out street car, a number of possibilities are available. The main objective of all of them should be to locate the engine and transmission as rigidly as possible. The simplest way to achieve this is to install solid mountings at both ends of the

Race cars which retain the stock floorpan, and some all-out street cars, make use of a rear transmission support which is tied into the roll cage, or a specially-fabricated cross member. This is a sure way to prevent the frame forks from flexing under load.

transmission. The problem with this is that the noise levels inside the car rise to what many may find unacceptable levels. However, if you plan on regular trips down the strip, this may be the best option. Of the solid mountings available, avoid using those with two separate mounting lugs at the bell-housing, choosing instead the type with a one-piece cradle to fit under the trans case. At the front end, by far the best design is the weld-in mounting manufactured by Gene Berg Enterprises which picks up on the four lower studs round the shift housing. This eliminates all possibility of snapping off the weak stock front mounting, a failure which has seen the demise of many a transmission over the years.

If you don't wish to raise internal noise levels too far, the solution is to use one of Berg's 'Super Duty' rubber-mounted assemblies. This also picks up on the four shift housing studs but includes a rubber-mounted cradle which is affixed to new mountings

welded to the frame horns either side of the transmission. With heavy-duty rear mountings and a traction bar under the rear of the engine (also available with a noise-reducing rubber pad), the engine and transmission won't be able to move anywhere, yet the car will not be anti-social in terms of noise levels inside.

As far as the clutch is concerned, there is no option but to use a 200mm assembly at the very least. It is also possible to use a 215mm flywheel from a later Type 2 (not to be confused with the

Cars which are destined to see street use should stay with the conventional clutch disc (on right) rather than making use of the competition-only feramic four-puck type. The latter are not designed to slip and can cause damage to the flywheel.

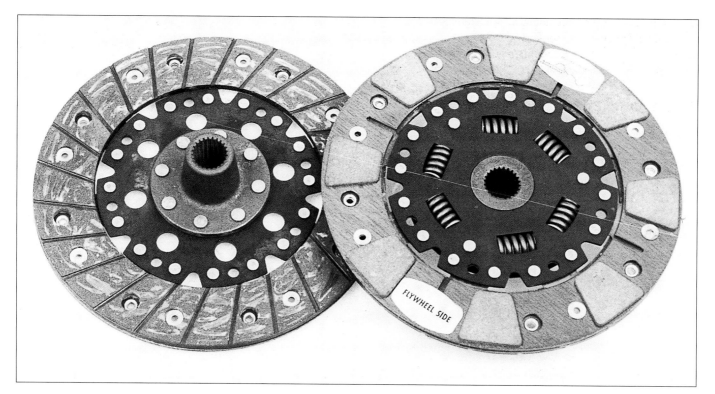

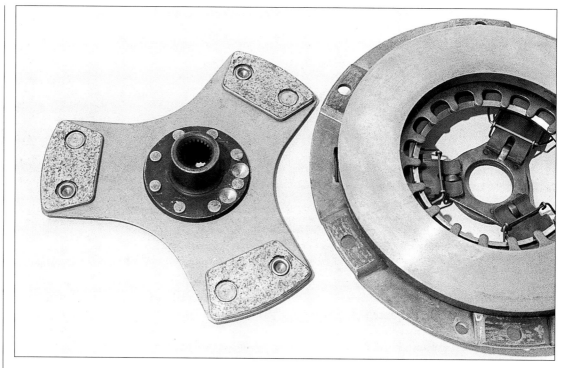

Berg's 'Super Street' clutch disc is interesting in that it features the use of two different materials on its friction surfaces. One side has a carbon type material, the other a space age composite designed to grip harder as it heats up.

While the three-puck disc on the left is not suitable for street use, the Berg pressure plate on the right certainly is – unlike most other clutches, this features a billet steel pressure surface which will not shatter like some cast-iron types.

bolt-on Type-4 style flywheel used on some Type 2s). With a 2300lb or a 2700lb pressure plate, the chances of suffering clutch slip are significantly reduced, even when using a stock-type center plate. While the pedal pressure will be significantly higher, it is not unbearably so. More recently, KEP have introduced a new range of pressure plates which, while having a high 'grab' pressure, do not require such a strong left leg to operate the clutch pedal. To cater for the increased clutch pressure, you must ensure that the cross-shaft is up to the job, as described in the fast-road section of this book. Failure to do so will almost certainly lead to

breakage, and sooner rather than later.

The two weaknesses of the stock-type clutch are the cover plate itself and the 'shoe' – the pressure surface of the clutch assembly. If a stock-type clutch is increased in pressure, the cover plate can warp. To prevent this, most quality cover plates have strengthening bars welded across them to prevent distortion. The stock shoe can shatter when subjected to extreme use as it is manufactured from cast-iron. Gene Berg Enterprises offers a range of heavy-duty clutches which have a shoe machined from a steel billet so as to prevent this problem occuring. As the company is also at pains to point out, cast-iron clutch shoes are not race legal, either.

You should not use three- or four-puck racing clutch discs on a street car as they are not designed to be slipped (such as when making a hill start or moving smoothly away from a stop light). If they are allowed to slip, they overheat, resulting in damage to the flywheel friction surface and pressure plate. A stock-style center plate should be adequate when used with a heavy-duty pressure plate on a street car running street tyres, but a Berg Super Street disc, with its composite/carbon materials, would certainly cure all problems.

SUSPENSION FOR THE ULTIMATE VW
How to enjoy the performance to the full

Much of what we have discussed with regard to a fast road car is applicable to an all-out street Beetle except that the necessity for modifying the stock suspension becomes greater with any significant increase in horsepower. Whereas you could get away with driving a 110bhp street VW with virtually stock suspension, when the engine's output climbs to 180bhp or more it really is time to take a look at things. After all, there is little pleasure to be gained from having an awesome motor if you cannot put it to good use.

Once we venture into the realms of ultimate street performance, we can begin to look at some more radical ways to improve the Beetle, although it is also necessary to be aware of the intended use to which the car is going to be put. Many cars at this level are aimed at weekend drag racing, with relatively few being built, other than in Germany, as out-and-out sports saloons. Where drag racing is concerned, there is relatively little attention paid to a car's ability to negotiate bends at speed – the prime consideration is to make the vehicle stable in a straight line.

Bearing this in mind, the areas to pay most attention to are caster angle, correct suspension geometry (toe-in/toe-out, front and rear) and dimensional accuracy. Caster angle has been explained in the previous fast road section, but just as important as far as directional stability is concerned is the matter of ensuring that the toe-in dimensions are set accurately.

On a Beetle, the factory settings for the front wheels are 2-4mm (0.08-0.16in) toe-in, unladen, while at the back the setting should be neutral. Some suggest running a degree or two of toe-out at the rear, although this can lead to some loss of stability at higher speeds. Others suggest that, on a Beetle which sees regular strip use, you should jack the front of the car up to a roughly level ride height, front to rear (assuming it normally sits nose down), and set the toe-in to zero. That way, when the car is accelerating, nose-up, there will be the minimum of drag from the front tyres. However, this is not conducive to good handling out on the street – it's

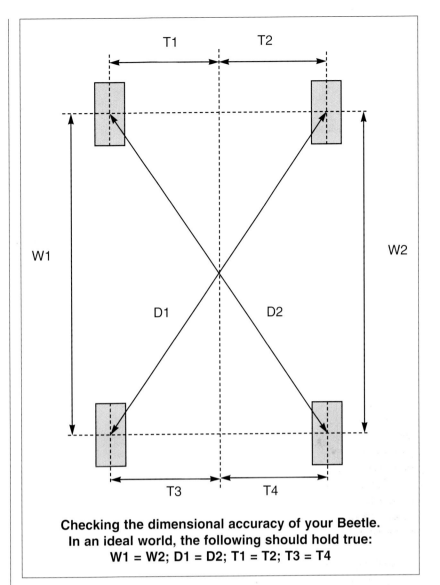

**Checking the dimensional accuracy of your Beetle.
In an ideal world, the following should hold true:
W1 = W2; D1 = D2; T1 = T2; T3 = T4**

all a question of what you want from your car.

With regard to dimensional accuracy, you should also check that the wheelbase is identical on each side – it is possible to have quite a variation as a result of removing and reinstalling the transmission a number of times without paying due regard to marking the exact positions of the axle tubes in relation to the spring plates. If you move one wheel forward slightly and the other back by a similar amount, you will have zero toe-in but at the expense of unmatched wheelbase dimensions. The only way you can check that all is well is to set the car up on axle stands and remove all four wheels. Drop a plumb line from the center of each hub and make a mark on the floor at the point where it touches. Now measure from left front to right rear and right front to left rear. These dimensions should be identical. Now check the wheelbase on each side. If they are also identical then all is well and the car is aligned perfectly.

If, however, the dimensions do not agree, side for side or corner to corner, then you have an alignment problem which may either be down to incorrectly set rear suspension or the result of accident damage to the axle beam or the chassis itself. If the wheelbase is equal on each side, but the diagonal dimensions are out, then it suggests that either the axle beam or the transmission is not centered in the car. To check this, you must establish an accurate center line – first, use the plumb line to establish the center line of the transmission by taking a plumb reading from the input shaft of the gearbox and marking the floor. Next, measure across the underside of the frame head of the chassis and find the center point. Drop a plumb line from that point and make a mark on the floor. Draw a straight line between the two new marks – this is your datum line from which other dimensions need to be checked.

Measure out from this center line to the marks you first made when taking readings from each hub. You will soon see if there is a major alignment problem. Unfortunately, if there is a deviation of more than 3-4mm (0.12-0.16in) then there may be accident damage which you will need to correct if your car is ever to handle correctly.

The matter of ensuring everything is perfectly aligned is especially important when you are involved with major surgery on a car, in terms of installing a new frame head or transmission mountings. Carrying out a frame head swap is something that may be worth considering if you run a Super Beetle, with MacPherson strut suspension at the front, but prefer to use a torsion bar axle so that you can install a lightweight glassfiber one-piece front end. Installation is relatively straightforward and it is the perfect opportunity to build in some added caster angle – trim the frame head and chassis as necessary to achieve the desired angle of inclination. You could also raise the frame head in relation to the rest of the car to lower the front end, with no loss of travel and with minimal effect on geometry. This may sound like radical surgery indeed, but it is nothing compared with what some people do when striving to produce the ultimate road-going Beetle.

Similarly, at the rear, it is possible to convert a swing-axle car to IRS by the relatively simple expedient of welding in the necessary brackets to support the semi-trailing arms. You will also need to change the transmission itself, the spring plates and the axles, etc. This conversion is more popular in Europe, where US-specification torsion bar front

with IRS rear chassis are relatively rare. The result is what many consider to be the best of both worlds.

Incidentally, when radically lowering the rear of an IRS Beetle, you will still end up with some camber changes, despite the IRS system being far less affected in this area than the alternative swing-axle design. To combat this, it is possible to swap the semi-trailing arms over from one side to the other, at the same time trimming off and swapping the shock-absorber mountings so that they are now below the trailing arms once more.

Another modification that can be made in the search for your ultimate Beetle is to raise the engine and transmission in the car, thus lowering it without inducing any camber changes at the rear wheels. This necessitates remaking the front and rear transmission mountings, although proprietary conversions are available which make this task far simpler. This modification is particularly popular on swing-axle cars which are to be used for some fairly serious drag racing, although there is no reason why it should not be carried out on a street car as well.

If you intend making adjustments to the ride height of your Beetle in the search for ultimate handling, you should install adjustable spring plates at the rear of the car. These spring plates allow you, at the turn of an Allen key, to wind the rear suspension up or down. This is very useful as it takes a lot of the hit and miss out of reinstalling torsion bars, as well as allowing you to pre-load one side of the car when running at the drag strip.

The torsion bars themselves should be upgraded, especially when using the car for some mild drag racing. The stock torsion bars are too soft to allow an efficient launch from the startline. Installing a pair of aftermarket 28mm torsion bars will make a world of difference, the original 22mm or 23mm bars being insufficient to cope with the rigors of drag racing. A car which is to be set up for improved cornering will also benefit from the installation of heavier torsion bars, although you will find that, at lower speeds, the ride will be much firmer – something you may wish to consider if the car is to be used for regular road use. Heavy-duty torsion bars should always be complemented by aftermarket shock-absorbers, as described previously.

BRAKE SYSTEMS
Bringing it all back to rest – quickly

With 180bhp or more on tap, you really do have to start thinking about ways to slow your VW down from speed, safely and efficiently. Many of the cars which fit into this category will have been built with a certain amount of drag racing in prospect, with braking efficiency far from the owner's mind. However, as anyone who has tried to slow a drum-braked Beetle down from 100mph at the end of the strip will testify, sometimes drag racing and braking systems do go together…

Installing Porsche 944 disc brakes on the front of your Bug is not a straightforward operation but it is definitely worth the effort. You will need to make up a special adaptor to mount the Porsche callipers, as not only are they a different design, but they also need to be mounted further out from the wheel center due to the larger diameter of the Porsche brake disc.

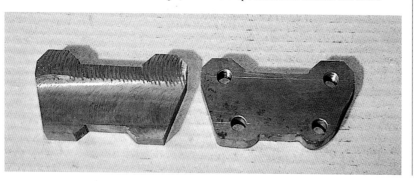

The stock calliper mounting needs to be spot-faced to give a flat surface for the new calliper bracket to locate on.

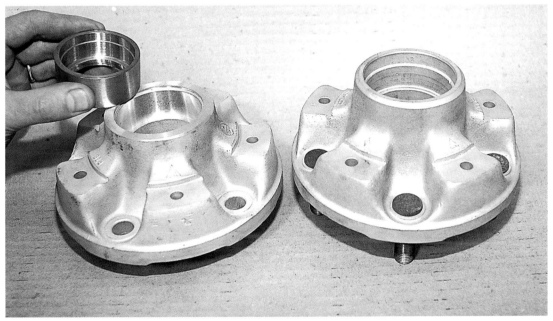

The Porsche aluminium hub must be modified to fit the VW spindles – the hub needs to be reduced in width and the bearing surfaces relocated as the inner and outer bearings are closer together on the VW spindle.

To support the outer bearing, you must make a small bushing which slips over the spindle and effectively increases its diameter. The outer diameter of the bush matches the internal diameter of the Porsche wheel bearing.

Once in place, the Porsche hub and disc assembly is located by the normal Volkswagen wheel bearing clamp. You will need to install the Porsche dust cover to prevent the bearings from running dry.

The new calliper bracket simply bolts onto the original calliper mountings – note the bracket bolts on to the rear side (hence the need to spot-face the mounting surface). Installation looks very neat and professional.

The Porsche brake calliper is far larger than the original Volkswagen unit and results in considerably improved stopping power when used in conjunction with the 944 ventilated brake disc, which is bigger in diameter than the original.

To install Porsche 944 rear disc brakes, you can use the Porsche cast aluminium calliper mounting, which simply bolts in place on the rear hub assembly of the IRS Beetle. You can also install the semi-trailing arms from a 944.

The splines inside the 944's hub match those of the Volkswagen stub axle. The hub slips straight on and is held in place with the usual 36mm hub nut, which must be torqued up to 217lbft (30kgm).

The 944 rear ventilated disc itself is a separate casting which is held onto the hub by a number of small screws. Bolt pattern is the traditional small Porsche 5-stud. Don't forget to install the split-pin in the hub nut.

For most people, the conversions described in the section on fast-road cars will suffice, but if you are planning on pushing your Bug to the limits, then you may wish to consider a more sophisticated set-up, such as adapting the ventilated disc brakes from a Porsche 944 to your Beetle.

While there are several aftermarket brake conversions available which, on paper at least, promise to deliver all the braking efficiency you are ever likely to need, the great benefit of the Porsche brakes is the use of ventilated discs. When used repeatedly, or from speed, brakes become extremely hot, this heat build-up eventually resulting in a total loss of effectiveness. Drum brakes are very bad at dissipating this heat, whereas discs fare much better. Yet even they cannot cope with hard use, the disc pads eventually becoming glazed over and less efficient.

To help combat this – and to improve their wet-weather performance – many people drill the brake discs, or machine grooves into them. Cross-drilling, as it is known, will make a considerable difference to the performance of an otherwise stock brake system but is not the ultimate solution. Major manufactures soon came to realise that there was another way to keep the brake disc cool and that was by making it partly hollow. This was achieved by making the disc thicker and casting a series of radial cooling slots within the disc itself. This allows air to circulate inside the disc, helping to dissipate

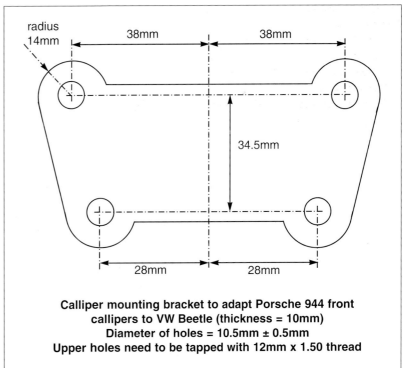

Calliper mounting bracket to adapt Porsche 944 front callipers to VW Beetle (thickness = 10mm)
Diameter of holes = 10.5mm ± 0.5mm
Upper holes need to be tapped with 12mm x 1.50 thread

the heat from within more rapidly.

Today, most production cars, and certainly all performance cars, come with ventilated discs as standard, their only drawback being that they can suffer from brake judder when very hot as the disc may show a tendency to warp.

German-made Kerscher front brake conversion features this high-quality ventilated disc which is designed to slip straight onto the stock Volkswagen disc brake spindles. The Kerscher disc doesn't require any modifications to the bearings.

Kerscher conversion uses this calliper which bolts onto the stock VW calliper mounting without the need for any adaptor bracket or machining. You can also upgrade the front brakes of your Bug by using Talbot Horizon front callipers.

Potentially, there are many ventilated disc brake systems which could be adapted to the Beetle, but the most popular has proved to be that from the Porsche 944 sports car. The 944, and its predecessor the 924, shared several components with various Volkswagens, including certain suspension parts. This led somebody in the past to take a close look at what could be swapped over from water-cooled Porsche to air-cooled VW, with the brake set-up coming in for particular scrutiny. Unfortunately, the system can only be readily adapted for use on a Beetle which has ball-joint front suspension and IRS rear.

The installation of the front disc assemblies

At the rear, the Kerscher brakes come with this cast aluminium hub seal retainer and calliper mounting. This bolts on in place of the original VW hub seal housing and is located with four bolts. Calliper mounts behind the wheel center.

Kerscher rear discs are not ventilated. They are manufactured in one piece and contain the necessary splines to match up with the VW axle. The conversion can be installed on a swing-axle Beetle, as shown here.

requires access to machining facilities as the stock VW stub axle has to be machined slightly to accept a mounting bracket for the calliper. The disc itself bolts to a separate cast-aluminium hub which will also need some machining to allow the use of a stock VW wheel bearing. On the 944, the inner and outer wheel bearings are further apart than on a Beetle, meaning that the hub needs to be put on a lathe and turned down slightly to allow the housing for the outer bearing to sit further in. Installing the large Porsche brake calliper requires the fabrication of a new mounting bracket, which is produced from 10.5mm thick steel, the dimensions of which are shown in the diagram on page 117.

Look carefully and you can see that the brake discs have been drilled on the front of this California Look Beetle. Drilling helps not only to keep the discs cool but also improves the braking efficiency in wet weather.

At the back, the installation is simplicity itself as the Porsche 944 semi-trailing arms can be installed on any IRS Beetle without modification, the only difference being that the 944 rear stub axle requires the use of the larger Porsche CV joint. The semi-trailing arms and other components even carry the VW and Audi logos! The calliper is supported on a cast aluminium bracket which forms part of the rear wheel bearing housing, while the ventilated disc is bolted to a cast steel hub.

An alternative to the 944 brake conversion is the four-wheel disc brake kit from Kerscher in Germany. This consists of ventilated front and plain rear discs, with callipers and all mounting brackets, and is of sufficiently high quality to satisfy even the strictest German test legislation. Installing the Kerscher kit on the front of a ball-joint Beetle is very straightforward: all you need to do is remove the stock disc assembly (or to install stock disc brake stub axles) and fit the new ventilated discs. The callipers supplied by Kerscher bolt directly to the VW mounting lugs.

At the back, the beauty of the Kerscher conversion is that it can also be installed on a swing-axle Beetle, although the rear discs are not ventilated. Once again the installation is very straightforward, requiring the removal of the original brake drum and backing plate, the bearing retainer and brake pipe. The kit comes complete with a new bearing retainer which incorporates the mounting holes for the brake calliper. Install the new brake disc and rear hub nut, followed by the calliper and brake pipe. Connect the parking brake cable and all that remains is to bleed the system and enjoy a new sense of security.

Both the 944 and the Kerscher conversions will effect a dramatic improvement in the braking abilities of your Beetle and allow you to make far better use of your car's performance and handling. As we have said many times, there is little point in increasing the horsepower if you cannot safely put it to good use. Engine, transmission, suspension and brakes – think of them as one package and enjoy the pleasure of driving a Beetle with the heart of a lion.

The Kerscher rear calliper has provision for a parking brake which connects up to the stock VW handbrake cables. The system is fully TÜV approved, meaning that it meets Germany's strictest safety requirements.

Complete conversion is neat and tidy – all you need to do is to connect up the brake pipes and bleed the system thoroughly to enjoy braking efficiency you only dreamed of. Four-wheel disc brakes on a Beetle are a worthwhile addition.

Wheels & Tyres

Aftermarket wheels which have been designed specifically for the Beetle, such as this EMPI 5-spoke replica, will give few problems regarding clearance and handling. Shod with 195/65 radial tyres, they look right at home on the rear of this cabriolet.

In the previous chapters of this book, we have made no specific recommendations regarding the choice of wheels and tyres for your mild street, fast road or all-out Volkswagen. The principal reason is that, in the vast majority of cases, owners tend to choose wheel and tyre combination on grounds of style rather than outright performance and handling expectations. For example, a full-house 13-second California Look sedan might produce in excess of 180bhp from its 48IDA carbed engine yet be equipped with classic 5in-wide BRM wheels with 135 and 185 Michelin radials. On the other hand, a mild 1641cc daily driver might drive around on a set of 6in wide polished Porsche alloy wheels with low profile tyres yet be capable of little more than 85mph.

However, by far the most commonly asked question when it comes to this subject is 'What size

In the USA, recapped slicks are street legal in some states. While offering tremendous grip in a straight line, they are not designed for extended street use as the sidewalls are so soft. A street tyre in name, if not in spirit!

wheels and tyres will fit my Beetle without having to modify the bodywork?'. There are no hard and fast rules about this as the matters of wheel offset and style come into play. Basically, you will be safe installing a set of 5.5in x 15in aftermarket wheels, such as the popular EMPI-replica 5- and 8-spokes, shod with up to 185/55x15 radials at the front and 195/65 radials at the rear. The reduced diameter of the front tyres will allow the wheels to turn without the tyres fouling the bodywork.

One of the most popular conversions will be to emulate the classic California Look, with 145x15 radials at the front and 165 or 175 radials at the rear, on anything up to a 5.5in wide rim. It is certainly possible to go narrower at the front – 135 Michelins have been a long-time favorite among the Cal Look crew – and wider at the rear: maybe even 195/60x15. It is all a question of what you are after with your car.

If ultimate straight line performance is your bag, with cornering speeds being low on your list of priorities, then 145 Michelins at the front with soft-compound 215/60 radials, such as Yokohama's A008 tyres, on the rear will get the job done. However, you will need wider rims to accommodate those 215/60 tyres safely. The author's street car is shod with 155x15 Michelins on 6in Porsche wheels at the front and 215/60x15 Fulda radials at the rear, this time on 7in rims. While the handling is hardly in the sports car league, it does corner far better than most California Look VWs with their skinny 135 tyres on the front end. Taking the straight line requirement still further, in the USA it is possible to obtain 6in slicks which have been recapped with a DoT-approved treaded compound for the ultimate blend of startline traction and street-legality. However, these recapped slicks are hardly what could be considered everyday street tyres.

There is a growing interest in what has become known as the German Look – a style where the car is built to resemble a competitor in the German Käfer Cup or French Super VW Cup race series. These cars look the business, with their 16in-diameter Porsche Cup wheels and ultra-low profile tyres, four-wheel disc brakes and race-inspired bodywork. With something like 225/50 (or even ultra-low 265/40) tyres, these cars can be made to

Forged aluminium wheels made by Fuchs have been used on Porsche 911s for years. They are high-quality wheels available in a variety of widths and diameters. Adapting a set to your VW will necessitate having the brake drums redrilled.

Replica BRM wheels by Flat Four in Japan have proved to be very popular. They are a shade over 5ins wide and fit any five-lug VW. This set has been bolted up to some Porsche 356B brakes – note the large polished aluminium drum.

Narrowing the axle beam allows you to tuck the front wheels further inside the fenders – this enables you to lower the front end a little more without creating any clearance problems. Mahle 'Gas Burner' wheels are relatively rare.

More and more people are fitting high-tech aftermarket wheels to their VWs in the search for an individual look. This custom Beetle has been fitted with 185/55 and 205/60 low-profile tyres on 7x15 three-spoke wheels – all under the stock fenders.

Larger diameter 16in wheels are particularly popular with proponents of the so-called German Look. These 225/60x15 radials fit under the stock fenders thanks to the Porsche 911 wheels having a fairly large offset.

handle like the race cars they emulate. In many cases, the use of these super-wide tyres and 16-inch wheels will require the fitment of widened fenders, be they flared in the style of the 1970s or widened by two or three inches. Much depends on the choice of wheel design and whether the car has been treated to some drastic suspension modifications, such as narrowing the front axle beam or rear end.

Narrowing the beam of a torsion bar Beetle has become more commonplace today than it was a few years ago when such tricks were the sole domain of

the drag racer. By cutting and shutting the axle beam, and trimming the torsion bars and tie rods to suit, it is possible to tuck the front wheels further under the arches to allow the suspension to be lowered more radically, or to enable wider low-profile tyres to fit without too many clearance problems. However, there is an increased risk of the tyres fouling the inner wheel arch, so be aware that while you may be solving one problem, you could well be creating another.

If there can be any such thing as a firm recommendation for a reliable everyday wheel and tyre combination which will improve the handling without recourse to costly ultra-low profile tyres, it would be to install those 5.5in-wide aftermarket wheels designed to fit a Beetle in the first place, shod with good quality 185/55 and 205/60 tyres. If you prefer a more conservative look, then 155 radials at the front with 185/70s at the back would make quite a difference, especially if used with a set of aftermarket shock absorbers.

As far as wheel choice is concerned, within reason it is possible to fit virtually any wheel to any VW – even the old 'wide-five' lug pattern rims to a later four-lug car – with the use of adaptors. However, we prefer to stay away from the use of adaptors as they can place a greater strain on wheel bearings, as well as considerably adding to the unsprung weight (the weight of the wheels/tyres/suspension/steering – the lower the unsprung weight, the better handling and more responsive the car will be). If you wish to fit wheels with a different stud pattern, it is preferable to have your existing hubs redrilled and a set of studs fitted in place of the original bolts. The most popular conversion in this respect is to redrill the hubs to the Porsche stud pattern, so that the famous Porsche 911 Fuchs alloy wheels may be fitted. On four-lug Beetles, the Porsche stud pattern is the same diameter as that of the VW, meaning that one of the original bolt holes can be used.

The best advice we can offer is to err on the conservative side when choosing wheels and tyres. Too skinny at the front will make the car understeer terribly, especially in the wet, while too wide will cause the steering to become very heavy. On Super Beetles, with their occasionally troublesome MacPherson strut suspension, the use of wide front wheels and tyres can lead to recurring wheel 'shimmy', which is hard to cure. In general, the rear tyres should be either the same size (unless you have fitted 135 or 145 radials) or slightly wider than those on the front. Don't go too extreme or you will once again help induce understeer.

The next time you are at a event, take time to wander round the show cars and have a look at the wheel and tyre combinations which most appeal to you. However, remember that, ultimately, it is you who is going to have to drive your car everyday, so choose wisely.

Engine formulae

ESTABLISHING COMPRESSION RATIO

To calculate the compression ratio (CR) of your engine, you need to know three things: combustion chamber volume (head cc), deck height displacement (that's the volume of the area above the piston at the top of the stroke) and the cylinder displacement.

$$\text{Cylinder displacement} \quad = \quad \frac{\text{Bore x Bore x Stroke x } 0.003142}{4}$$

$$\text{Deck height displacement} \quad = \quad \frac{\text{Bore x Bore x Deck Height x } 0.003142}{4}$$

Combustion chamber volume (head cc) is measured using a calibrated syringe or, in the case of many aftermarket heads, this figure can be supplied to you by the cylinder head manufacturer.

$$\text{CR} \quad = \quad \frac{\text{Cylinder Displacement + Deck Height Displacement + Head cc}}{\text{Deck Height Displacement + Head cc}}$$

For example:
Bore = 90.5mm; Stroke = 82mm; Deck height = 1.5mm; Head cc = 46cc therefore:

$$\text{CR} \quad = \quad \frac{521.66\text{cc} + 9.65\text{cc} + 46\text{cc}}{9.65\text{cc} + 46\text{cc}} \quad = \quad 10.37{:}1$$

ENGINE CAPACITY CHART

STROKE (in mm)	BORE (in mm) 83	85.5	87	88	90.5	92	94
64	1385	1470	1522	1557	1647	1702	1777
69	1493	1585	1641	1649	1776	1835	1915
74	1602	1699	1760	1800	1904	1968	2054
78	1688	1791	1855	1897	2007	2074	2165
82	1775	1883	1950	1995	2110	2180	2276
84	1818	1929	1997	2044	2161	2234	2332
86	1861	1975	2045	2092	2213	2287	2387
88	1905	2021	2093	2141	2264	2340	2443

CHOOSING CARBURETTOR SIZE AND JETTING

$$\text{Carb size} = \frac{\sqrt{(\text{cc per cylinder} \times \text{maximum rpm})}}{40} \qquad \text{Choke diameter} = \frac{\text{Carb size} \times 40}{50} \qquad \text{Main jet} = \text{Choke diameter} \times 4$$

For example: 2160cc engine = 540cc per cylinder; Max rpm = 7,000rpm, therefore:

$$\text{Carb size} = \frac{\sqrt{(540 \times 7000)}}{40} = 48.6\text{mm} \qquad \text{Choke diameter} = \frac{48 \times 40}{50} = 38.4\text{mm} \qquad \text{Main jet} = 38 \times 4 = 152$$

(a 48 IDA Weber or 48DRLA Dell'Orto would be suitable in this instance)   (a 38mm choke would be ideal)   (A 150 or 155 main jet would be a good starting point in this instance)

These can only be considered ball-park figures, necessary to get the engine running sufficiently well for break in. At the earliest opportunity, you should have the carburettors set up accurately on a rolling road or dyno.

CRANKCASE CODE LETTERS (implemented 8/65)

Code	cc	Type	Dates	Notes
A	1200	Type 1	up to 7/65	(1192cc 30bhp)
B	1600	Type 2	8/67 - 7/70	
		Type 1	8/68 - 7/70	(USA)
C	1600	Type 2	8/67 - 7/70	(M240)
D	1200	Type 2	from 5/59	(1192cc 34bhp)
		Type 1	from 8/65	(1192cc 34bhp)
E	1300	Type 1	8/65 - 7/70	
F	1300	Type 1	8/65 - 7/70	
G	1500	Type 2	up to 7/65	
H	1500	Type 2	8/65 - 7/68	
		Type 1	8/65 - 7/70	
		Type 181	8/69 - 2/71	
K	1500	Type 3	8/65 - 10/73	
L	1500	Type 2	from 11/65	
		Type 1	8/66 - 7/70	(M240)
M	1500	Type 3	8/65 - 7/73	
N	1500	Type 3	8/65 - 7/73	(M240)
P	1600	Type 3	8/65 - 7/73	(M240)
R	1500	Type 3	8/63 - 7/65	(1500S)
T	1600	Type 3	8/65 - 7/73	
U	1600	Type 3	from 8/65	(fuel-injection)
UO	1600	Type 3	8/67 - 7/73	
AB	1300	Type 1	8/70 - 7/73	
AC	1300	Type 1	8/70 - 7/75	(M240)
AD	1600	Type 1	8/70 - 7/73	
		Type 2	8/70 - 7/73	
AE	1600	Type 1	8/70 - 7/71	(USA)
AF	1600	Type 1	8/70 - 1/80	(M240)
		Type 2	8/70 - 7/79	(M240)
		Type 181	1/74 - 1/82	(M240)
AG	1600	Type 181	8/70 - 7/76	
AH	1600	Type 1	8/71 - 1/76	(USA)
AJ	1600	Type 1	8/74 - 12/80	(USA & Japan fuel-injection)
AK	1600	Type 1	8/72 - 7/73	(USA)
AL	1600	Type 181	3/73 - 7/79	
AR	1300	Type 1	8/73 - 7/75	
AS	1600	Type 1	8/73 - 7/80	
		Type 2	8/73 - 7/79	

(Note: M240 = Optional Low Compression Engine, a reference to the type of piston installed)

Transmission Codes

(All refer to Type 1 Beetle unless otherwise marked)

CODES	MODEL	FINAL DRIVE	REMARKS
AA	1200	4.375	From chassis No 0 981 810
AB	1300	4.375	Up to 8/70
AC	1500	4.125	Also some 1300 from 8/70
AD	1200	4.375	Limited Slip Differential
AE	1300	4.375	Limited Slip Differential
AF	1500	4.125	Limited Slip Differential up to 8/70; also some 1300 from 8/70
AG	1200	4.375	Type 147 (Fridolin)
AH	1500	4.125	IRS suspension from 8/68
	1600	4.125	8/69-8/72
AK	1500	3.875	Type 181 Trekker up to 8/70
	1600	3.875	Type 181 Trekker from 8/70
AL	1500	3.875	Type 181 with LSD up to 8/70
	1600	3.875	Type 181 with LSD from 8/70
AM	1300	4.375	Saloon and Cabriolet from 8/70
AN	1600	3.875	Karmann Ghia with IRS from 8/70
AO	1600	3.875	Karmann Ghia from 8/70
AP	1300	4.375	Limited Slip Differential from 8/70
AQ	1600	4.125	Limited Slip Differential 8/70-8/72
AR	1600	3.875	Karmann Ghia with LSD from 8/70
AS	1600	3.875	Type 1 from 8/72
AT	1600	3.875	1303S and Cabriolet from 8/72
AU	1600	3.875	Ditto with LSD
BA	1300/1500	4.375	Semi-automatic from 8/68-8/70
BC	1300/1500	4.375	Ditto with LSD
BE	1600	4.125	Semi-automatic from 8/70-8/71
BF	1600	4.125	Ditto with LSD
BG	1300	4.125	Karmann Ghia semi-automatic from 8/70
BH	1300	4.125	Ditto with LSD
BJ	1300	4.375	Semi-automatic from 8/70
BK	1300	4.375	Ditto with LSD
DA	1500/1600	4.125	Type 3 swing-axle up to 8/68*
DB	1500/1600	4.125	Ditto with LSD*
DC	1500/1600	4.125	Type 3 with IRS from 8/68
DD	1500/1600	4.125	Ditto with LSD

* Note that reinforced swing-axle design was available on post-8/68 Type 3 models as an option (M263).

GEAR RATIO FORMULAE

$$MPH = \frac{RPM \times \text{Tyre Diameter (in inches)}}{\text{Drive Ratio} \times 336}$$

where Drive Ratio = (Ring & Pinion ratio) x (Gear Ratio)

For example, with a tyre diameter of 25ins, a final drive ratio of 4.125 and a top gear of 0.89, the road speed at 5,000rpm would be:

$$MPH = \frac{5000 \times 25}{0.89 \times 4.125 \times 336} = \frac{125,000}{1233.54} = 101.33mph$$

Changing the formula around,

$$RPM = \frac{MPH \times \text{Drive Ratio} \times 336}{\text{Tyre Diameter (in inches)}}$$

Using the data from the previous example, at 70mph:

$$RPM = \frac{70 \times 0.89 \times 4.125 \times 336}{25} = \frac{86,347.8}{25} = 3459.9rpm$$